Touching The Earth

TOUCHING THE EARTH:
The power of our inner light to transform the world
Dharma Talks by Seon Master Daehaeng

First Edition: May 2015
English translation and editing by Hanmaum International Culture Institute
Published by Hanmaum Publications
Cover Design by Su Yeon Park

© 2015 Hanmaum Seonwon Foundation
All rights reserved, including the right to reproduce this work in any form.

within Korea
tel: (031) 470-3175 / fax: (031) 470-3209
outside Korea
tel: (82-31) 470-3175 / fax: (82-31) 470-3209
e-mail: onemind@hanmaum.org
www.hanmaumbooks.com

Printed in the Republic of Korea

ISBN 978-89-91857-34-6 (03220)

국립중앙도서관 출판시도서목록(CIP)

Touching The Earth : the power of our inner light to transform the world / Dharma talks by Seon Master Daehaeng ; English translation and editing by Hanmaum International Culture Institute. -- [Anyang] : Hanmaum publications, 2015
  p. ;   cm

Translated from Korean
ISBN 978-89-91857-34-6 03220 : US$16.95

225.2-KDC6
294.34-DDC23   CIP2015011631

Touching the Earth

THE POWER OF OUR INNER LIGHT TO TRANSFORM THE WORLD

Dharma Talks by
Seon Master Daehaeng

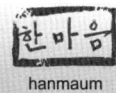

hanmaum

Contents

6   Foreword

8   About Daehaeng Kun Sunim

12   The Spark That Can Save The Universe

44   The Infinite Power Of One Mind

66   In The Heart Of A Moment

94   One With The Universe

112   Protecting The Earth

144   Glossary

Foreword

You are connected to every thing and life in the universe. Don't believe me? Try doing anything on your own. The food we eat, the air we breathe, all of it comes from this interconnected whole. One sip of air is a billion lives in your body working together. Each step on the floor is gravity working with you.

All of the energy, creativity, and insight of the universe is flowing together with us. Right now. It's there for the taking, free for anyone to use. And no matter how much you use, it will never run out. When we begin to live in accord with this connection – call it one mind, the foundation, God, or Buddha-nature – this energy and wisdom can flow through us. This connection is there within each of us, calling for us to pay attention.

At the point where we meet this connection, all realms – visible and invisible – are connected as one. This is the interpenetrated flowing of everything, both seen and unseen. When we rely upon this, the energy of the whole will respond to us and infuse our acts. The decisions we make will be more complete, and the actions we take will be more harmonious because we can feel their effects in the people around us.

The very first step is to simply begin relying upon this connection. It exists within each of us. Like oxygen, it's there and it is what sustains us. Begin by entrusting it with the things that come up in your life. Take the questions you have and ask them there. Observe what comes back out, observe what you experience, and then look for ways to put that into practice.

Doing this, your experiences will deepen and you'll begin to see the world as if for the first time.

Don't settle for just knowing. If you do, it will fade into a happy memory, with no power to help anyone. Application, on the other hand, has the power to blow your mind. Application can show you ways of thinking and doing that you could never have imagined. Application will make you cry with joy at the simple ways you've changed your thinking. Just be sure to keep entrusting everything you know and don't know to this inner Buddha essence. Let it all go back there, and you won't get caught up in fixed ideas or attachments about your experiences.

One of the implications of this interconnectedness is that our potential is much greater than we realize. As Daehaeng Kun Sunim explains in the talks that follow, there are no "big things" or "small things" in this whole. Nothing is separate; it is all "myself." Learning to open ourselves to this connection, we begin to realize that we have the power to help comfort those who are hurting, and to free those who are stuck. Even the problems of the world and environment are not beyond our grasp. In offering us these Dharma talks, Daehaeng Kun Sunim has truly set us upon the Bodhisattva's path.

May all beings discover the light within them, and may they share it with the world.

With palms together,
The Hanmaum International Culture Institute

About Daehaeng Kun Sunim

Daehaeng *Kun Sunim*[1](1927-2012) was a rare teacher in Korea: a female *Seon(Zen)*[2] master, a nun whose students included monks as well as nuns, and a teacher who helped revitalize Korean Buddhism by dramatically increasing the participation of young people and men. She broke out of traditional models of spiritual practice to teach in such a way that allowed anyone to practice and awaken, making laypeople a particular focus of her efforts. At the same time, she was a major force for the advancement of *Bhikkunis,*[3] heavily supporting traditional nuns' colleges as well as the modern Bhikkuni Council of Korea.

Born in Seoul, Korea, she awakened when she was around eight years old and spent the years that followed learning to put her understanding into practice. For years, she wandered the mountains of Korea, wearing ragged clothes and eating only what was at hand. Later, she explained that she hadn't been pursuing some type of asceticism; rather, she was just completely

---

1. Sunim / Kun Sunim: Sunim is the respectful title of address for a Buddhist monk or nun in Korea, and Kun Sunim is the title given to outstanding nuns or monks.
2. Seon (Chan, Zen)**:** Seon describes the unshakeable state where one has firm faith in their inherent foundation, their Buddha-nature, and so returns everything they encounter back to this fundamental mind. It also means letting go of "I," "me," and "mine" throughout one's daily life.
3. Bhikkunis: Female sunims who are fully ordained are called Bhikkuni(比丘尼) sunims, while male sunims who are fully ordained are called Bhikku(比丘) sunims. This can also be a polite way of indicating male or female sunims.

absorbed in entrusting everything to her fundamental *Buddha*[4] essence and observing how that affected her life.

Those years profoundly shaped Kun Sunim's later teaching style; she intimately knew the great potential, energy, and wisdom inherent within each of us, and recognized that most of the people she encountered suffered because they didn't realize this about themselves. Seeing clearly the great light in every individual, she taught people to rely upon this inherent foundation, and refused to teach anything that distracted from this most important truth.

Her deep compassion made her a legend in Korea long before she formally started teaching. She was known for having the spiritual power to help people in all circumstances with every kind of problem. She compared compassion to freeing a fish from a drying puddle, putting a homeless family into a home, or providing the school fees that would allow a student to finish high school. And when she did things like this, and much more, few knew that she was behind it.

---

4. Buddha: In this text, "Buddha" and "Bodhisattva" are capitalized out of respect, because these represent the essence and function of the enlightened mind. "The Buddha" always refers to Sakyamuni Buddha.

Kun Sunim saw that for people to live freely and go forward in the world as a blessing to all around them, they needed to know about this bright essence that is within each of us. To help people discover this for themselves, she founded the first *Hanmaum*[5] Seon Center in 1972. For the next forty years she gave wisdom to those who needed wisdom, food and money to those who were poor and hungry, and compassion to those who were hurting.

---

5. Hanmaum[han-ma-um]: "Han" means one, great, and combined, while "maum" means mind, as well as heart, and together they mean everything combined and connected as one. What is called "Hanmaum" is intangible, unseen, and transcends time and space. It has no beginning or end, and is sometimes called our fundamental mind. It also means the mind of all beings and everything in the universe connected and working together as one. In English, we usually translate this as "one mind."

Daehaeng Kun Sunim founded ten overseas branches of Hanmaum Seon Center, and her teachings have been translated into twelve different languages to date: English, German, Russian, Chinese, French, Spanish, Indonesian, Italian, Japanese, Vietnamese, Estonian, and Arabic, in addition to the original Korean. For more information about these or the overseas centers, please see the back of this book.

The Spark That Can Save The Universe

This Dharma talk was given by
Daehaeng Kun Sunim on December 17, 1995.

December 17, 1995

Even though you all came here for today's talk, many of you are sitting out in the cold because the new Dharma Hall still isn't finished. I can't tell you how bad I feel about this. Both you and I came here for the Dharma talk, so we should be able to share the same warm room. I'm so sorry not to be able to provide at least this. We all express ourselves in different ways, but this sensation of cold and discomfort is the same for each of us.

Even though the physical circumstances are somewhat difficult, there aren't many places like this, where people can learn to focus directly on their fundamental *mind*[6] and develop that potential. Further, I have no doubt that the sincere faith and efforts of practitioners here in Korea have planted innumerable good seeds, and that the spiritual ability and strength of everyone, both sunims and laypeople, are ensuring that these roots of goodness continue to be planted.

---

6. Mind (心)(Kor. –maum): In Mahayana Buddhism, "mind" refers to this fundamental mind, and almost never means the brain or intellect. It is intangible, beyond space and time, and has no beginning or end. It is the source of everything, and everyone is endowed with it.

The Inner Buddha, Dharma, and Sangha

Practitioners here sometimes say that they're relying upon the *Three Treasures*[7] that exist within themselves, don't they? When you hear this, you probably have a pretty good idea of what it means. However, when I refer to our inherent nature as "my unmoving foundation," this may seem like a strange expression. I describe it this way because our foundation doesn't actually move; instead, it provides the energy that allows things to move. It's like the axle of an old-fashioned cart: it remains very stable, and so makes it possible for the wheel to move. Like this, our foundation always remains very calm and quiet, yet it sends forth great energy. Through this energy, everything in the universe is ceaselessly working and changing, beyond time and space, without stopping for even a millisecond.

You may wonder why I repeat this point so often. I keep bringing it up because many of you have only an intellectual understanding of it. You've mistaken theoretical knowledge for actually connecting with this deep essence that's within you [pointing to her heart]. You're trying to make things happen by using your head and moving your body, instead of communicating the situation to this place deep inside and then acting from there. This is such a shame, and it's why I keep repeating myself — if you understand only a little bit, then I also

---

7. Three Treasures (三寶)**:** In their outer aspect, the Three Treasures are the Buddha, the Dharma, and the Sangha. Buddha means both the historical Buddha, as well as this fundamental enlightened essence. Dharma means both ultimate truth, and the truth taught by the Buddha. Sangha in its broadest sense means the community of great practitioners, both lay and monastic. These are also considered to have an inner aspect as well.

only understand a little bit. If you know this much [holding her arms wide], then I also know that much! If you are a great ocean, then I also am a great ocean.

So, this inwardly existing *Buddha, Dharma,* and *Sangha*.[8] can be described as thus: 1) The unmoving source of infinite energy, the foundation of our present consciousness; 2) the raising of thoughts from this foundation; and 3) the movement and functioning that result from these thoughts. These are also Buddha, Dharma, and the Sangha. Thus, taking refuge in the Three Treasures also means taking refuge in yourself. This is because the Three Treasures all exist within our inherent nature.

PRECEPTS, SAMADHI, AND WISDOM

Then, what about keeping the *precepts*, practicing *samadhi*, and gaining *wisdom*?[9] How are these attained and practiced in the context of relying upon these inner Three Treasures? As I'm always saying, everything is coming directly from your inherent nature: it's you, true self, that's receiving and producing everything; it's you that's moving this body; it's you that's seeing; it's you that's hearing; it's you that's going and coming, that's eating and excreting, sleeping and waking up. It's you that's doing every single thing. A tree has its root, and is alive because of that root. Our every movement happens because of our root.

---

8. Buddha, Dharma, Sangha: (see footnote 7)

9. Precepts, Samadhi, and Wisdom (戒定慧)**:** Traditionally described as the Threefold Training, these are aimed at putting an end to desire, hatred, and delusion. Precepts represent virtue and morality, samadhi represents transcendental awareness, and wisdom is this awareness in action.

So, no matter what you confront, if you focus everything on one place — your fundamental mind — this becomes true samadhi, precepts, and wisdom. This is what's called the "fragrance of precepts, samadhi, and wisdom."

Approach everything by entrusting it to your fundamental mind; then, you won't end up causing problems for yourself, your teacher, the temple, or your fellow practitioners. This is how sunims practice as well. If you do something that causes problems for yourself, that action also ends up causing hardships for your entire family, doesn't it? If one person in a family gets involved in something negative, the entire family feels it, including their parents and children.

So, view everything that confronts you as something that you helped create. No matter whether it comes from outside or arises from inside, whether it's good or bad, unconditionally accept it as something you have made. Even when you clearly know who or what caused those troubles, view them as something you've made, and entrust the whole situation to your foundation. Don't blame your husband, don't blame your wife, don't blame your children, and don't blame your parents. Entrust it all as something that you've caused. Whether things are going well or badly, you experience everything that's happening in your life because you are here. Now, some of you are saying, "Why should I blame myself when I didn't do anything wrong?!" However, think about this: Because you exist, others exist. If you weren't here, how could others' actions affect you? This is why I say to take everything as something that you have made.

If you take everything as something that you've created, and then let it go deep within you, such that it connects with your foundation, later it will come back out as something new. When you connect with your foundation like this, what you input comes back out according to the intention you input it with and has the power to move the material world in that direction. But when your thoughts just spill out of your mouth, this connection isn't made.

For this reason, people who are determined to realize their foundation hold their tongues and become quiet. They return every single thing inwardly and entrust it all to their foundation. Having been deeply input in this way, those situations are communicated into their foundation, and through this they manifest back into the world in a changed form. When people input the things they encounter like this, those things all change for the better; thus, nothing they encounter can hinder or derail them. What could oppress you when everything you entrust to this spiritual dimension is sent back into the material realm in a more harmonious form?

However, when problems occur, many people just react directly to those, and run around looking for solutions in the material realm. Unless you first entrust things to your foundation, nothing will go right. You'll lose your direction, accidents will happen, and you'll get caught up in hatreds and feuds. The minds of some of those around you will become darker and darker, and leading a normal life will become impossible. Do you think you can solve all of these things through your intellect and sweat? When you're able to truly return and entrust everything you encounter to your foundation, such that what you input changes and manifests back into the world, then your life will become very relaxed and many problems will cease to be.

All lives and things in the universe are connected with each other, communicating heart to heart. Do you know why this is?

Within your body right now is every level of existence that you have ever experienced, as you've evolved over billions of eons. There's nothing in the universe that you haven't been, and all of those same forms exist within you right now: every single one of those is "me."

You might think that you have secrets unknown to anyone else, yet in the unseen realm of the Dharma, there are no secrets. I use the expression "unseen realm of the Dharma," because we can't see it with our physical eyes, and yet through it, every single thing is always freely communicating with everything else. Secrets may exist in the material realm, but in this nonmaterial realm, everything is known. Because nothing is secret, because nothing is withheld, every single thing you do is automatically recorded within your foundation. Everyone desperately needs to know this.

The Fragrance of Spiritual Practice

"The fragrance of the precepts" means taking everything that arises — from within you or outside of you, whether it's something about your family or your job or whatever — and returning it all to your foundation. In this way, the situation will manifest in a more harmonious, healthy form. When you can do this, you'll feel at peace with yourself and all other people as well.

However, if you speak without restraint about every little irritation, "She is so difficult!" or "That son of a ....!" this will actually make things worse for you than if you had made the effort to work things out harmoniously. Through the karmic connections created over innumerable lives, you and everyone else are all one family, so should you really be behaving like this? If you continue to think and act harshly towards each other, when will this cycle ever end? So take everything and input it harmoniously into this inner foundation; handled in this way, it will manifest harmoniously back into the material world. That which comes back out will have the power to move the world. It will protect you, it will smooth out the rough spots in your path, and it will give you opportunities to solve whatever difficulties you encounter, allowing you to move forward freely.

When you can thoroughly entrust everything to your foundation, and can remain focused on this foundation in all the things you do, this is called "the fragrance of samadhi." At this point, what I call the "pillar of mind" has firmly taken root within you, so you remain unshaken in any circumstances. Thus, if you are able to realize the "fragrance of samadhi," the "fragrance of precepts" isn't difficult. When you return everything inwardly like this, keeping the precepts isn't a problem.

However, without doing this, it's impossible to uphold even the five basic precepts. Please think carefully about this. Do you think you can keep the five precepts without entrusting everything inwardly? These are the precepts of not drinking alcohol, lying, stealing, engaging in improper sexual behavior, or killing. If you're not trying to do things through your fundamental mind, if you're not acting from that place and inputting into that whatever arises, then you won't be able to keep even these precepts. When you return everything inwardly, to your foundation, you'll realize that others' lives are also your life, so you won't intentionally do anything that harms others. Returning things like this also ends up saving you from harm as well.

Nevertheless, if your mind wanders around after external things, you can't deeply enter into this meditative awareness, and so the pillar of mind isn't able to become completely grounded. This lack of a secure footing damages your ability to receive and send out everything through your fundamental mind.

When this pillar of mind is unsettled, you become scared and nervous when you encounter difficulties. There's an underlying nuance of fear and confusion that pervades your experiences, whether it's something arising from the inside or the outside, or whether it's a problem with your children or your parents. Everything about your fundamental mind, *Juingong*,[10] will seem more vague and confusing. "I called out to Juingong, but nothing happened." Should I laugh or cry when people say things like this? You have to firmly raise this pillar of mind, and completely grab hold of it. If you can do this, then the thoughts you give rise to will naturally be input, and will manifest into the world.[11] Even though you may have been coming here for years,

---

10. Juingong (主人空): Pronounced "ju-in-gong." Juin (主人) means the true doer or the master, and gong (空) means "empty." Thus Juingong is our true nature, our true essence, the master within that is always changing and manifesting, without a fixed form or shape.

Daehaeng Sunim has compared Juingong to the root of the tree. Our bodies and consciousness are like the branches and leaves, but it is the root that is the source of the tree, and it is the root that sustains the visible tree.

11. You have to input unconditionally and harmoniously, with the well-being of all in mind. If you're trying to input while still clinging to some desire or fear, or with greed or hatred, things won't go well for you, nor will your pillar of mind become grounded.

if your pillar of mind isn't deeply settled, your practice may be no more developed than that of someone who has been coming here for a few months. If this applies to you, what should you do about it? What should you do to grow and deepen your practice? Wouldn't it be nice if you could solve this with your intellect? But this isn't something that belongs to the realm of thoughts. Nonetheless, some of you are doing exactly this, and think you know everything about our fundamental mind. Just because you have some ideas about it doesn't mean that you truly know the real thing.

You all probably know someone like this: they feel confident in their thoughts and opinions about what I'm teaching, and so think that they've truly reached that level. They mistake thoughts for experience and the ability to apply that experience. As time goes by, they gradually stop coming to the temple. However, when problems arise, they struggle and squirm, because they haven't made any effort at putting their understanding into practice. They don't know where they've come from or where they're going. They lose their direction, and don't know how to handle the things in their life. How could such a person engage in the spiritual practice that can swallow the entire universe, as well as the Dharma realm, and the past, present, and the future?

If you're aspiring to practice, you have to first thoroughly ground yourself in relying upon and entrusting everything to your foundation. Living with a family is the same way: only when you are deeply settled in your role and responsibilities will your family be harmonious and peaceful. If your attention is always somewhere else, how can your family thrive?

Like this, the lives within your body also need to be firmly settled and working as one. They need to be rooted in this. Then there will be a deep quiet and peace that will naturally bear fruit. When this fruit ripens, you will be able to give it to others as well. Even though you give it to others, your center remains just as it is.

To put it another way, the seed of Buddha remains just as it is, so you'll be able to completely send out and receive everything through your foundation, using every kind of wisdom and profound ability. Only when you can do this, can it be said that you are in the state of samadhi.

Samadhi means that you are completely rooted in this foundation. So, everywhere you go, that is your place, every person you see is also yourself, the pain you witness is your own pain, and even insects are your own body. Every single thing is yourself, so compassion naturally arises for them all. This isn't forced or artificial, it is utterly genuine compassion.

When we see something, thoughts arise, and according to those thoughts, we move and act. This is "receiving and sending forth." Now, the question is this: are we doing this from our foundation, with wisdom, or are we doing it from our head and our intellect? The corresponding results will be as different as heaven and earth.

If you're unable to rely upon your fundamental mind, and instead try to use your intellect to handle everything, the harm to we humans, to the planet, and even to other planets will be incredibly serious. What is true on the human scale is also true on the universal scale. Even the stars in the sky shed their shells when the time comes, and only their essence remains. After this essence is sifted out, it's born anew through a black hole. This process is exactly the same as what we experience at the human level.

Do you realize that there are definite reasons why you've encountered this practice of learning to rely upon your fundamental mind? This spiritual practice isn't something that you can do just because you want to, nor is it something that you can quit just because you want to. There is a very deep principle that has led you to this practice. In this difficult era, all of you were given the assignment of taking care of everything through your fundamental mind. This is neither planned nor accidental. It has arisen from the karma and affinities that you have created as you've evolved over billions of years. So you must not avoid practicing, giving one excuse after another.

Then, how should you handle things? When something happens in your family, for example, you, your children, your parents, and even the lives inside your body should all become one through your foundation. If all become one mind, energy radiates outward and helps take care of people's minds. To explain it one way, once all those minds become one through the foundation, it's as if they all become condensed into an extract. When this condensed essence bursts forth from the nonmaterial realm into the physical realm, it takes the form of material energy that can function in and affect this realm. Sometimes, there are problems so severe that even working through our foundation, one or two people alone can't take care of them. At those times, many people all together have to entrust the situation to their foundation; then those problems can be solved.

If the situation calls for the *Bodhisattva*[12] of Compassion, this energy becomes *Avalokitesvara*.[13] If the Bodhisattva of Manifestation is needed, it becomes *Ksitigarbha*.[14] When people need the Seven Star Spirit, the Dragon Spirit, or the Earth Spirit, our foundation manifests as such. Your foundation freely manifests in whatever form or manner is necessary. That energy doesn't all have the same form or "wavelength." According to the need, it changes and splits in an infinite variety of ways, and functions in harmony with the circumstances.

In order to fully use your fundamental mind like this, you must have realized the "fragrance" of the precepts, samadhi, and wisdom. You must further realize the spiritual state that we call the "fragrance" of being able to help free beings from attachments and ignorance. Beyond this is the level where you can manifest as needed, freely going back and forth among the past, present, and future as the occasion demands, manifesting as anything. Only when you have reached this state, that of the *Tathagata*,[15] can you handle the solar radiation of the sun, as well as the problems of other stars, black holes, and the universe.

---

12. Bodhisattva: In the most basic sense, a Bodhisattva is a manifestation of Buddha, which helps save beings and also uses the non-dual wisdom of enlightenment to help them awaken for themselves.

13. Avalokitesvara Bodhisattva (觀世音菩薩): The Bodhisattva of Compassion, who hears and responds to the cries of the world, and delivers unenlightened beings from suffering.

14. Ksitigarbha Bodhisattva (地藏菩薩): The guardian of the earth who is devoted to saving all beings from suffering, and especially those beings lost in the hell realms.

15. Tathagata (如來): In one sense, Tathagata is just another name of the Buddha, meaning "Thus-come," but it also refers to the fully enlightened state that is able to both know and manifest with complete freedom.

PREDICTIONS OF THE FUTURE

When I was about eighteen or so, I first heard stories and predictions about the end of the world. However, as Sakyamuni Buddha said, "Just seeing isn't the Way. Focusing on seeing and making prophecies, while lacking the ability to change things, is the act of a small person." Being able to hear everything, yet remaining unable to resolve things, is not the Path. The power to hear everything is not the Path. The power to know the minds of others is not the Path. The power to go anywhere without moving your body is not the Path. And the power to know past and future lives is not the Path. Instead, the Path is found within the letting go of all attachments to those kinds of powers. You have to be completely free of all of these kinds of powers, then you'll be able to perceive everything and to take care of everything. At the stage where you are not caught by those, you can freely use them as needed. You can receive anything, and send forth anything. No matter how much you send forth, your foundation doesn't shrink, and no matter what or how much you receive, it doesn't increase.

So who are these people that are making prophecies? One person you've probably all heard of is Nostradamus. As you know, he predicted all kinds of different things. However, these sorts of prophecies aren't the words of a person who has realized the truth. They aren't the words of someone who has mastered and is unattached to the *five subtle powers*,[16] and who can use his or her

---

16. The five subtle powers (五神通): These are the power to know past and future lives, the power to know others' thoughts and emotions, the power to see anything, the power to hear anything, and the power to go anywhere.

fundamental mind to respond to any need. When someone who practices relying upon this fundamental mind becomes aware of future events, they immediately start working on that situation, and so prophecies about those events become worthless. You really need to engrave what I'm saying in your heart.

There was a man who could ride clouds, and who was always traveling around here and there. One day a great practitioner perceived that the man was nearby, and decided to follow him and see what he was up to. The practitioner saw that the man was doing all kinds of bad things, and so he stopped him from being able to ride the clouds. Do you know why I'm telling you this? Because events that people like Nostradamus expected to be the apocalypse have already come and gone several times. People who make these kinds of predictions can't hold a candle to someone who has awakened to their fundamental mind and knows how to live from that place. When such people see a crisis approaching, they deeply input into their foundation the thought that we should not fall into chaos or go extinct. Even though such a disaster is facing us, if we all input the thought that we and the planet should live together in harmony, it will be so. Please give this a try.

You already know that the surface of the Earth is always changing, don't you? It's always opening, crashing together, rising or falling, and changing direction. But if you could lead these changes so that they happen gently, then what would there be to worry about?

The land and all beings move because they are alive. Dirt is alive, water is alive, rocks are alive; everything is moving because it is alive. So even if someone predicts a cataclysmic disaster in China, Japan, or the U.S., if you can guide the ground so that those changes happen gradually, without large disruptions, what is there to worry about? In this way, human beings can find a way forward. This is why predictions about the end of the world have no meaning. The words, "the end of the human race," have no relevance in the varied and ever-changing panorama of life. Why? Because life arose from earth, water, fire, and air, and from those, countless beings evolved, including human beings. They live and evolve because the material basis of the four elements and the seed of Buddha-nature have always been present. These have never disappeared. So don't be bothered by talk that the world or civilization will be destroyed on such-and-such a day. If people work together through their inherent foundation to harmoniously and wisely take care of whatever arises, then even the destruction of the earth can be averted.

The Power and Compassion that Arises from Spiritual Practice

People usually say there's no life on planets like Mars, Venus, Jupiter, and Uranus, don't they? However, if there is water or soil, this will create air, and life will form. There are forms of life that live in even boiling water; even this can sustain and give rise to life. This profound and boundless truth is also called the Buddha-dharma. People can't imagine just how vast and how subtle this word is. The Buddha-dharma isn't limited to a particular religion or something that only Buddhist monks or nuns can study. From a bug to a blade of grass to the four elements, everything is Buddha.

According to their circumstances, those tiny living things began to change over time. They began to feel suffocated with the way they had been living and aspired to something better. In this way, they began to evolve and change. They got tired of walking around on four legs, and wanted to try walking on two legs, and so it happened. We even have the spot where the tail was attached. Like this, all of the shapes of your past lives are within your body even now. This is so profound.

People have many different skin tones, don't they? There are people with very white complexions, there are people with reddish complexions, with black complexions, and with yellowish complexions. These are all the results of people living in different environments, which also led to natural differences between regions. On top of this, how people react to the things in their life causes them to gather together with people who have similar *karmic affinities*.[17] In the fullness of time, that karma manifests in the area where those people have gathered, and affects everyone there. Through this process, the "healthy" ones are selected, and the rotten ones are sent to the compost pile, so they can have a chance to start over. This is why, once in a while, you see such terrible catastrophes in certain areas, where it seems like nearly everyone starves to death, or is burned to death. This all happens as a result of the choices people have made and how they've reacted to things, to put it a bit bluntly. It's you that makes yourself pitiful, and it's you that can make yourself better. After this sorting, it's also you who decides where you'll be born again. Death is not the end.

Nonetheless, you should still help those people who are suffering and in pain as they are caught up in these changes. Do

---

17. Karmic Affinity (因緣)**:** The connection or attraction between people or things, due to previous karmic relationships.

not dismiss their suffering, thinking "They deserve it; it's all the result of their own bad behavior." Understand how this world works, and realize that others are also a part of yourself.

Don't limit your compassion to just those who are suffering. Include even those who are behaving very badly; try to examine why they first did those things, and then direct your kindness there. If you keep raising such a kind and generous mind, when you come back into this world, it will be as a truly great person who is able to do much good for everyone. Don't neglect to give food to those who are hungry, nor comfort to those who are suffering.

By the way, if the Earth were to fall into disaster, not only would this cause serious trouble for human beings, it would also cause a lot of problems for the universe as well. Disasters on the Earth will lead to great upheavals in other places. It's necessary to be flexible and respond with wisdom to ensure that these things don't happen. For example, if there are too many people in one place, then we can take measures to help them live in a more spacious area. If we, as citizens of the world, put our minds together to address the problems we face, we can take care of anything.

Things have now reached the stage where the Earth has become so worn out that if we can't repair it, we'll be watching helplessly as we die. So, what do we have to do? Ultimately, all the work we do has to be done through our fundamental mind. If we aren't doing it through our fundamental mind, no matter how hard we try, we won't be able to repair the Earth. And even if we somehow managed to make some repairs through ordinary means, there would be no energy to sustain those repairs. There would be no way to survive. Without being able to use our fundamental mind, we will not be able to absorb the energy that exists in the empty space all around us.

Without including this fundamental mind, scientists who study this kind of energy will be unable to truly make progress in their research. Thus, those people who practice relying upon their fundamental mind have to become one with scientists in order to help lead them to solutions that will benefit all of humanity.

Mind functions without limitation, so it can become a hundred, a thousand, or ten thousand. It has no fixed essence, so it takes countless shapes and moves in an infinite number of different ways. Because it never remains the same for even an instant, names are meaningless, nor can we truly speak about anything we've done. So, when scientists are working on a particular area of research, if we raise the intention that their work should go well, then the energy of that combines with them and helps their research move forward. If we keep raising and sharing the energy of our foundation in this way, we'll achieve the infinite and incredibly powerful Dharma. It is utterly without limitation, and is subtle and profound beyond imagining. Through it the blind can see and the lame can walk. Truly, it can guide and sustain the entire world.

Yet, if we think, "There's nothing we can do about it," or "If that happens, human beings will be wiped out," then that's what will happen. Don't ever get caught up in the idea that some sort of apocalypse is coming and so you should hide deep underground in caves or bunkers. If you plan on trying to survive by storing up a few months or years of food and living underground, you'll end up being reborn as a burrowing insect or rodent.

Besides, does "under the ground" really have any meaning? Imagine the Earth as it floats in space. Even though you go into the ground, from this perspective, there's no difference between being on the surface or under it. There's no use in trying to live under the ground. If something is wrong with the planet, how much good is burrowing a few inches under the surface going to do you?

So don't let the fear of death cause you to waste your time with such trivial ideas. Instead, you need to come to know your eternal, true self. This true self exists. It is a single seed that can feed the entire world. It remains just as it is, without shrinking or decreasing, and can feed the whole world forever. We must each experience this incredible truth for ourselves, and make it our own.

Steadfast Faith in Our Inherent Nature

One day, an older man came and told me about his experience with this practice. He'd been feeling ill for a while, and so went to the hospital. The doctor told him that basically everything was wrong with him: he had diabetes, jaundice, problems with his heart and liver, and so forth. Further, the doctor said that because of his age, there was nothing that could be done for him. The doctor suggested that he be admitted to the hospital, where they could ensure that he'd sleep well. Essentially, he should just stay in the hospital until he died.

Because he was in a lot of pain, the doctor gave him an injection, and that was all he could do for the old man. The old man started crying because, looking forward, his life seemed so pointless. Through his tears he said to himself, "Juingong! True self! You created this body, and it's you that's causing it to hurt so much. So if I'm supposed to die, then let's get it over with! If you need me to live, then let me live. Suit yourself!"

He then left the hospital and went home. To himself, he said, "It seems like this body has become worn out and useless, so let's change it for a new one right away. Anyway, true self, take care of this in whatever way is best." He spent several days with this attitude, when suddenly the pain vanished. This happened because his entrusting was very sincere and so was able to connect with his fundamental mind, which is connected to all the parts of his body. His intention was communicated throughout his body, where those lives began to put it into action. Because of this, his pain disappeared and he was able to start eating again. A while later, when he was feeling much better, he returned to the hospital. His doctor was amazed, asking him, "How are you still alive?!"

Inherently, we cannot say that this is "my" body, because it is actually a collection of countless different lives. So wouldn't it be nice to completely let go of the thought that it's "my" body, and just live together peacefully? Is there any need to struggle so hard to avoid death? Listen: if you are someone who truly believes in your root, your foundation, then after you shed your body, not only will you take another birth right away, but you'll also be born as a great being.

Nonetheless, people are so reluctant to take off their old clothes,[18] and instead cling desperately to those worn-out

---

18. Clothes: In Korea, the word "clothes" is often used to describe our body. Like our body, they are something we take off at night (i.e. death), and then replace with a fresh set in the morning.

threads. If you can completely let go of all clinging to those, how relieved you'll be! Suppose you were dying right now, and were leaving behind five or six young children. You'd still have no choice. You'd have to let go of even that worry and regret, and just go. So live while letting go of absolutely everything, as if you were at the moment of death, exhaling your last breath.

Let's live without creating attachments. Love as much as you want to, but do it while not clinging to the other person. Live as good a life as you want to, but do it without clinging to your body. People become scared of dying, and so flee to a hospital where they experience terrible hardships and undergo all kinds of surgeries. Why are they so flustered with terror? Why do they have to cut their old clothes to ribbons before they can finally let go of them? No matter how old and discolored your clothes are, isn't it still easier to take them off while they're intact?

My overall point is this: people who want something more out of life shouldn't allow themselves to be drawn outward by the things that happen to them. Instead, they must take everything that confronts them and return it inward. Even though you have a good intellectual understanding of what I'm saying, please, please don't mistake that for true understanding. Instead, have firm faith in your inherent foundation, and entrust every single thing there. No matter what confronts you, your practice needs to be such that when you quietly entrust something to your fundamental mind, that which you entrusted will change and manifest back into the world. Your understanding and practice have to be translated into action. Only then will you be able to truly deal with all the problems of your family, the Earth, and the universe.

Questioner 1(male): Hello. I came here today to share my experiences of having late-stage lung cancer. Hopefully others may find something useful in what I experienced.

About three years ago, I began to feel pain in the left side of my chest. I went to see a doctor, but he couldn't find anything wrong with me. A week later, the pain returned, so I went to a larger hospital for a full check up. They thought I might have tuberculosis, but when the results came back, everything was fine. So I just carried on with my life as usual. It was about three months after this that I became very sick and had to be hospitalized for two weeks with pneumonia.

A couple of months after that episode, I suddenly felt a terrible pain deep down in the left side of my chest. I immediately went to the emergency room and was admitted to the hospital, where I spent a week undergoing all kinds of tests. Meanwhile, I was so nervous that I was constantly smoking. When the results came back, the doctor wouldn't say anything to me, nor would my wife. When I finally got her to talk to me, she broke down into tears and choked out the words, "It's cancer."

Hearing this, it felt like my brain had been disconnected from my body, or that I was in the middle of a nightmare; nothing around me seemed real. I had never thought that cancer was something that could affect me; it was a disease that happened to other people. I couldn't stop crying and asking, "What will happen to our two young sons? I'm only thirty-three. There are still so many things I want to do. Why is this happening to me?" Everything seemed so unfair, and I was filled with rage. No one who hasn't experienced this can understand what I felt as I sat there crying and crying.

The next day, the director of internal medicine referred us to one of the best chest surgeons in the country, so we went to see him for more detailed tests. The test results confirmed the details of the cancer, and a date for surgery was set. The day before the surgery, I had a full-body CAT scan. Suddenly, that night I was told the surgery would have to be canceled. The cancer had spread to my brain, and there was no point anymore in having the surgery.

My last chance was radiation. It lasted twelve days, and was so painful. My hair fell out, I lost ten kilograms, and I couldn't eat anything. After examining the results, my doctor wasn't hopeful. He said that with the cancer spread to the brain, we couldn't expect much benefit from chemotherapy drugs, either. He felt that no matter what he tried, I only had about three more months to live. With so little time, and so little hope, he said there was no point in continuing such painful treatments.

Now there wasn't even the faint hope provided by these treatments. All I could do was wait to die. I was completely stunned. After leaving the hospital, my wife and I cried all the way home. My mother-in-law had come to help look after our sons, and after we told her the news, she too started crying wildly as soon as she looked at our nine-month-old son. We were so lost and hopeless, and it was so hard just to get through each day.

My older brother was living down in the countryside at our family's traditional home, and he called and suggested we come down there because the air was quite clean. As we were getting ready, one of his neighbors called me and told me about you (Kun Sunim) and Hanmaum Seon Center. So my wife and I came to see you at the Anyang main temple. You told us, "Work hard at learning how to entrust everything to Juingong, your foundation, and observe without any clinging. Have firm faith in your essence, Juingong, for that is doing everything!" When we visited you again sometime later, you repeated the exact same thing.

At first I didn't know what entrusting was, nor did I understand anything about Juingong. It was only after quite some time and a lot of reflection that I began to have a feeling for what "Juingong" meant. I realized that Juingong is the foundation within me, and the foundation of the entire universe as well. As I practiced and experimented, I also discovered that this place within me called Juingong is what handles all of the things that confront me. I came to know that it is Juingong that gives rise to illness, and it is Juingong that causes illness to disappear. So I started completely entrusting everything to Juingong, and relying upon that place.

The pain got really bad several times. On those occasions, I would go visit the Hanmaum Seon Center that was near my brother's home and tell the abbot about it. He once said something that I've never forgotten: "Don't worry. Just entrust the pain to your Juingong. Before you knew anything about your foundation, you were in pain because you were becoming sicker. Now that you understand about this foundation, the pain is arising because you are getting better. So just keep entrusting it to your foundation." I tried to set down my fear, and entrusted the pain to Juingong, thinking, "This body is yours, so what happens to it is up to you."

When I would do this and relax, there would come a moment when the pain would completely disappear. Even when I was overwhelmed with the fear of dying, I entrusted that to my foundation. I've been doing this for the last three years. The doctors told me I wouldn't last more than three months, and yet I've been able to survive for more than three years. As I've entrusted everything to this foundation, Juingong, I've worked to view everything positively, and to live with a clean and open heart. Through this, I've come to realize that everything is achieved through this inner, fundamental mind. I've really been serious about relying upon this mind. When I was in pain, I kept entrusting that to Juingong, again and again.

These days, I'm very healthy, and the doctors say that there is no sign at all of the cancer. I have no doubt that this is the result of me relying on and entrusting everything to my foundation, Juingong.

I'd like to say to everyone here: Be relentless in relying upon your foundation! Let's be crazy about our fundamental root, Juingong! Without a doubt, Juingong is there, underlying everything. I would like to also express my endless gratitude to Kun Sunim, the other sunims, and all the many people who have helped me and my family. Thank you very much.

Kun Sunim: Like I said before, we can change everything, not just disease, because the essence of our mind is ceaselessly changing and manifesting according to the thoughts we give rise to.

Questioner 2(male): From my own experiences with practicing, I have come to know that we have to let go and entrust everything to this fundamental mind, including even overwhelming or humiliating things. This summer, it felt like I was able to let go of everything without having to think twice about it. It felt like simply tossing something into a wastebasket. However, one thing that I've noticed is that when I've entrusted something and it has gone well, there is a clean and clear feeling about it. But, when things haven't yet been resolved, I notice this feeling is missing. I'm wondering if it's because my faith is a bit weak, or is that just the way things work? Is this feeling missing because the process just isn't finished yet?

Kun Sunim: When a company hands a task to a trusted employee, they forget about the problem and move on, don't they? However, when they have to give a task to someone who is less experienced or trustworthy, then they have to continually keep checking up on that person. This very same thing applies to what you're asking about. It's a sign that you aren't thoroughly and completely believing in your foundation. If you completely believe in your foundation, then even if the sky falls, you're not worried. Even life and death issues don't bother you because you know that your inherent Buddha-essence will take care of things for the best. The words "completely believe in your foundation" hint at a power that words can't contain. There is a deep power in water as it finds its place, although its flowing is calm and serene.

Like this, when your faith has become deeply rooted in your foundation, even dying won't scare you. The prospect of death won't frighten you a bit. This is because you know that this inner master is what is taking care of everything that confronts you, and that your ordinary consciousness and body are just errand boys for this Buddha within us.

Questioner 2: When I react to the things in my life without first specifically trying to entrust them to my foundation, do those thoughts, words, and actions become my karma?

Kun Sunim: [shaking her hand from side to side] If your practice of relying upon your fundamental mind is very settled, you can take care of everything even while watching TV. You can handle things in the unseen realm while doing other things in the material realm. When you truly believe in your fundamental mind, entrusting and observing isn't a separate, intentional thing. If you're already aware that everything is being done by this root, why should you need to separately entrust things? When you're completely aware that your foundation is doing everything, you already naturally entrust everything as soon as it comes up. When someone needs to repeatedly keep saying, "True self, only you can do this. You take care of it," they're still at the beginning level, and their trust in their fundamental mind hasn't completely settled down.

Even though it sometimes looks like I'm just sitting around not doing anything, this fundamental mind [placing her hand on her chest] is moving and working very powerfully. Just go forward naturally from the place of your foundation. As you do things, sometimes you'll feel grateful, so, feel grateful and go forward naturally. If you don't feel grateful, that's not a problem; just go forward naturally. When you feel grateful, go ahead and express that. For example, "Ah, Juingong, thank you so much! Thank you for taking care of everything in my life. Thank you for all the lessons and the Dharma you've taught me." When something arises naturally like that, it's very authentic, very real. When I say, "don't get too caught up in trying to intentionally or forcefully entrust and let go," this doesn't mean to suppress something when it's spontaneously arising.

Questioner 2: Thank you.

Kun Sunim: The previous questioner spoke for quite a while about his experiences and his suffering, but even though people may talk for a long time, please don't think "Enough, already! Let's get on with the Dharma talk!" Listening to other people's experiences is also part of your practice. You may find a phrase or word that really touches your heart and helps your practice go forward. It's all practice, and it all can be a guide that shows you the way.

Questioner 3(male): Kun Sunim! Today I am truly greeting you!

Kun Sunim: [laughs] So, the other times you were faking?

Questioner 3: The last time I was so clueless! Anyway, I really wanted to see you today. Also, I wanted to let you know that I'll be retiring soon.

I had an interesting experience as well. I've been practicing asking and speaking to my inner nature, and from inside I heard, "If you go to the Seon Center and see Kun Sunim today, the sprout will break through." Could that really happen? [Audience laughs.]

Kun Sunim: Go on, I'm listening.

Questioner 3: After I started talking with myself like that, I started learning from within myself. It's amazing!

Actually, how I first came to the Seon Center amazes me as well. I'd never heard of the Seon Center or the principle of one mind. However, one day I heard about your talk at the KBS Hall in Ulsan City, and decided to go. Right after the talk, I happened to pick up three different issues of the old Hanmaum Bulletin. I kept them in my pocket, and for months I read them over and over again. I'd been reading and thinking about what they were saying for about six months, when a Hanmaum Seon Center opened in Ulsan. All of this really instilled the feeling that I needed to practice and awaken to this fundamental mind, as well as the feeling that, through this foundation, I needed to do a better job of taking care of the people in my life. I don't have a particular question today, but I am curious about what "the sprout will break through" means. I can only guess it means that something good will happen.

Kun Sunim: In the sutras, Sakyamuni Buddha gives the example of a house that's on fire. The house was burning, but the children were playing inside, with no idea of what was happening. Their father was outside and wanted to save them, but he was afraid that if he yelled "fire," they would panic and run further into the house. So he called out to his children, "Children, come here. Let's go and buy you some wonderful toys!" Of course, the children came running, and were saved. Although this can be described as an example of skillful means, used to encourage the children to come outside, it was also something that spontaneously arose from his foundation.

Likewise, when you have deep faith in your foundation and just jump directly into what's confronting you, even though you don't understand what's going on, your foundation responds very straightforwardly – "Okay." The one that's responding like that is the one that's responsible for getting things done; it's the one that can take care of things. In a similar sense, what you heard about the sprout is your true self reminding you it's there. Take this experience as an opportunity to deepen your faith and your spiritual practice.

Questioner 3: As I've listened to your Dharma talk today, about half the things I wanted to ask were answered or suddenly resolved. Thank you, I feel so relieved!

Kun Sunim: Wonderful!

It is most urgent that you know for yourself just how wonderful your own root is. Your root is so great, and is the only thing that can truly lead you. Never forget this! Jesus once said that those who don't believe in "me," and instead believe in others, would fall into a pit of demons or become a plaything for goblins. He was saying that we have to believe in the divine essence within each of us, but this was mistaken for believing in Jesus himself.

Here's what I think: the truth Jesus realized is the same as the truth the Buddha realized, which is the same truth that you all are living in the middle of. The truth through which the entire world functions exists everywhere and applies to all of us. Regardless of whether ten thousand people or ten million people awaken, they all realize the same truth. It is this truth through which every single thing in the universe functions.

Yet although everything functions together as one, even in this, there is nothing fixed or unchanging. This means that even the truth that everything functions together as one is empty. It continuously flows, changes, and manifests anew; there is nothing about it that you can grab onto or label. This is also how everything and everyone functions. So entrust everything you do to your foundation; entrust everything you experience, everything you see and hear. Entrust all of this while letting go of any thoughts of entrusting. If you can truly believe in your root like this, you will certainly come to know your root. Practice like this, and be diligent about it!

A long time ago, I watched a stream flowing for the entire day. The stream didn't say anything to me, so I waited and watched for three days more. It's hard to believe how stupid I was back then! That said, sometimes you need such stupidity when you want to discover and learn to rely upon your fundamental mind. Please, everyone, really try to practice hard. If we lived for only this one lifetime, I probably wouldn't tell you any of this. However, we repeatedly go through life after life. So we have to practice! This world is the middle realm; its purpose is to sift out beings and send them on to higher or lower realms. Now is the time for us to be diligent and leave this realm for the upper realm — the upper realm that transcends all labels such as "upper realm."

Thank you all for coming. Let's stop here for today.

The Infinite Power Of One Mind

This Dharma talk was given by
Daehaeng Kun Sunim on April 20, 1986.

April 20, 1986

Meditation Applied to Our Lives

Deeply settle your minds and listen carefully. If you're not calm, if you're not settled down, you can't take the direct route (pointing to her chest).

What we're talking about today isn't just theory or philosophy. If you're serious about spiritual practice, then you need to have steady faith in your true nature, Juingong. You must always entrust everything to that place, and go forward relying upon this foundation in everything you do. After entrusting, take what comes out and entrust that to your foundation as well. Again and again, you have to keep returning everything to your foundation. This is the meaning of meditation, and is meditation in action. Do you know why I keep bringing this up whenever we meet? Because if you do otherwise, nothing you do will truly benefit yourself, nor will it have any benefit for the other beings living with us on this ship we call the Earth.

As we humans have examined the world around us, we've given names to all the plants, animals, and inanimate objects. From this activity, diverse fields of study have gradually arisen, such as biology, philosophy, engineering, literature, politics, and medicine. Even hundreds of years ago, this process had generated a huge amount of theoretical knowledge about the world and how we should live. However, it wasn't put into practice, and so people lost sight of what is very fundamental to us. Because of this, we have been slow to develop the spiritual side of things, and people have suffered terribly over the centuries.

If we can just use the abilities inherent within every human being, our future and the level of our existence will change. So take what we're talking about and apply it to all the things that arise in your daily life. By doing this, the energy of your practice will spread to others, and your words and actions will become manifestations of the Dharma. Further, in addition to applying this practice to your daily life, you have to apply it to all beings, both living and dead, as well as to the inanimate world. You must apply your practice toward developing the universe as well as yourself.

People tend to believe only in what they can see with their eyes, so when something abruptly changes, they no longer recognize it. Both people and things take on one shape, and then put on another shape, and still yet another. People talk about things like "living" and "dying" because they don't know the reality: that it is all changing, every single instant. Inherently, there is no living or dying, because everything is only changing its shape and moving from here to there. Thus, ultimately, birth, death, karma, cause and effect, and rebirth all happen according to the thoughts you give rise to. Sometimes it's even said that these things don't exist, because everything is changing every instant. Nothing remains behind for birth and death, cause and effect, and even karma and genetics to stick to.

I learned this long ago when I lived in the mountains. One day after an icy snow covered the mountains, I found that the road I was on had become very slippery. What's more, it was heading downhill and becoming very steep. It was like walking on glass, but I found that if I took very short, fast steps, I could work my way down it. However, if I hesitated and stood still for even a moment, I would immediately begin to slide sideways, and would fall down. I had to keep my feet moving; they couldn't remain motionless. Our lives are just like this: we have to be able to move with the ever-changing nature of the world.

Undiscovered Gifts

Later, as I reflected upon this experience, I suddenly realized that we have within each of us all of the powers of evolution and creation, which makes it possible for us to be constantly moving and changing, and to even change our shapes. Likewise, we are also endowed with the five subtle powers. These are the ability to see everything everywhere, the ability to hear everything, to travel without moving one's body, to know past and future lives, and to know others' thoughts. For example, the ability to hear everything can also be called the power of communication. However, these days, we use phones and radios. Likewise, people use telescopes to substitute for our inherent ability to see everything in the universe. We are all endowed with these kinds of abilities, but we are unable to properly use them. It can honestly be said that we are missing fifty percent of ourselves.

However, if we understand the principles of how the world works — the principles of our fundamental mind — then the missing fifty percent is filled in, and we are able to properly use all one hundred percent. This is living Buddhism, which fills people with energy and awakens them to the worth of life. When spring comes, everything comes alive and blossoms naturally. The azaleas, forsythia, and magnolias all send forth flowers; every kind of plant turns green, the frozen ice melts, and the valleys fill with bubbling streams and singing birds. The Buddha's Pure Land is also attained like this.

If we understand this principle and can continuously apply it as we go through life, it becomes a great tool for us. It's as if we have our own magic wand. With a wave of it, everything becomes possible. This place where everything becomes one — one mind — is the essence of the Earth, of the sun, and of the very universe itself. It's so incredible! This magnificent one place, this one single point, produces everything. It's where everything is connected. It can give, do, support, embrace, and turn things around. Your own fundamental mind can do all of this!

So take this one place, this one mind, and try to skillfully apply it to everything. By "skillfully," I mean returning your thoughts and feelings inwardly, as opposed to directing them outwardly. If you return all of these things inwardly, *"one thought"* [19] will naturally arise from there, and within that "one thought" is the power to change and develop even the universe. If you can practice like this, the entire universe exists right there, in your daily life, and as you take care of your daily life, you also take care of the universe. How could this work be anything other than sacred?!

---

19. One Thought: This refers to the ability to raise and then input and entrust a thought to our foundation. When we can connect with our foundation like this, then through our foundation, that thought spreads to everything in the universe, including all of the lives in our body. At that instant, because all things are fundamentally not two, they all respond to that thought.

I hope that you will listen carefully to what I'm saying, and won't dismiss it as just some lecture. What I'm talking about are the things that happen to us every day, and what we have to do to truly solve those. If I tried to give you clever or easy-to-follow Dharma talks, they would just be dead words. They would have no power to help you. When you're thirsty, you need water that you can drink right away. So, I'm trying to give you teachings that are useful and adaptable to your daily life, teachings that will help you grow and go forward.

From time to time, problems will occur in some country, or around the world, where an event throws everything into chaos. To me, those kinds of problems aren't difficult to solve. The will of one mind, which combines all the minds of the entire universe, works to sustain the Earth. It even causes all kinds of negative energies to dissipate. All of the ups and downs we go through as we practice are the preliminary steps that will eventually enable us to go forward peacefully and harmoniously, as one mind. Using what you've learned, you can help even the universe develop.

As I said earlier, when something changes, when it is moved from here to there, people have no idea what happened. It's like not noticing that the larva became a cicada, or that the cicada becomes the larva. Likewise, most people are unaware that we human beings, too, have been constantly moving from one form to another and evolving.

Nonetheless, we've managed to develop quite a bit by relying upon things like genetics, and, by using this knowledge, to change plants and animals to increase production. But if we examine this at a deeper level, matter itself exists because of the unseen aspects of the non-material realms. From this arose what scientists call our genome, as well as all material things. Thus, this unseen aspect, what I sometimes call the *mujeonja*,[20] can cause DNA and genes to function or not function. This is due to the fundamental power of this unseen aspect, as well as its ability to communicate with everything. So, as I mentioned before, when everything becomes one and functions together, that unseen aspect has incredible power to cause things to arise or to expire. Whatever confronts you, the unseen aspect can swallow it and convert it into positive energy and nutrients. You all have this incredibly helpful power within yourselves.

If people around the world raise their level of consciousness and apply this to their daily life, then everything about our lives can change, even the form of our bodies. Our future would completely change. For example, these days you're dependent upon machines when you want to use energy or to communicate with someone, but imagine a world where this could all be done by simply giving rise to a thought. This is the kind of future I'm talking about.

---

20. Mujeonja [/mu-jun-ja/]: The essence, or medium, that connects the material and non-material realms and allows them to function together harmoniously. It is the underlying essence that allows the balanced functioning of the non-material realm and what is manifested into the material realm. To put it another way, we call it something that allows the spiritual realms to freely interact with the material realm. If it had a physical essence, it couldn't perform this role, so it could be said that it belongs to the non-material realm. However, it is within the physical realm that the functioning of the mujeonja manifests, so we cannot say that it belongs to one realm or the other.

When the mujeonja manifests into the material realm, it works through a phenomena called "yujeonja"[/yu-jun-ja/]. Its movement gives the appearance of infinitely tiny threads, but it is so small that it's impossible to detect any mass. It's this yujeonja that gives rise to everything in our physical world, and makes it possible for everything to function and interact.

Don't let yourself think that this is impossible. If you think of yourself as poor, then truly, you will become poor. If you think of yourself as well-off, your life will be deeply prosperous. So don't let yourself get caught up in thoughts of poverty or sadness. Try to live an enthusiastic and meaningful life. Be humble. And face things with a smile.

When you put this wisdom into action in your daily life, not only will your life become happier and more prosperous, but you'll also be able to make a huge contribution to the well-being of the world and the universe. This is how we become more than people who just speculate about the reality of our world. By putting the Buddha's teachings into practice like this, your words become the truth and manifest into the world. Try this for yourself. See what happens when you put this into practice.

Take a look at history. People have given rise to great civilizations, but in many cases these couldn't continue for long, and now only exist as a few broken buildings. Looking at these cultures, you may wonder why they declined, and what led to their development. All of this was the result of how those people used their minds.

When we look at the people who played important roles in the development of a certain place, we can see that they were focused on how to improve the lives of their fellow citizens, at least initially. But as time went by, they or their culture turned their focus outward, towards material things. This was unfortunate, because we need to always be returning everything to our foundation. Then, while functioning as one from that place, we automatically become one with everything we encounter. However, instead of doing this, they tended to compare themselves to others or to blame others, and this gives rise to desire, resentment, hatred, and eventually to fighting. It's only a matter of time before such a civilization collapses.

As an enlightened being once said, "If you entrust everything that confronts you to your fundamental mind, without blaming others, then I will return here." If you keep returning everything to your fundamental mind, how could Buddha or Jesus exist apart from you? How could you be any different from the people who developed those great cultures and civilizations?

Everything depends upon our fundamental mind. We all have such incredible potential within us. If you were born as a human being, it's already latent within you. For example, you're already endowed with the ability to see everything, to know others' thoughts, to know past and future lives, to hear everything, and to go anywhere without moving your body. Nonetheless, most people see only shadows of their true self. Because they don't see what's essential, they are easily led down useless paths. Spending all of their time and energy struggling with these, they never develop the great abilities inherent within themselves.

On the other hand, if we know how to freely use these abilities, we can cause great flowers to bloom across the nation and the world. Our culture and our future will all change, and even our ideas of space exploration will change.

Let's compare these subtle, inherent abilities to machines such as telescopes, telephones, computers, movie projectors, and so on. The five subtle abilities have these same qualities, except that they function automatically. When you return a thought to your foundation, it circulates there, and then goes to the brain where it's sent out. This is done automatically. But instead of trying to rely upon this fundamental mind, people get caught up in discriminations. They argue about Buddhism and Christianity, and fight over all kinds of ridiculous things. Those people they would look down upon are really no different than themselves. Throughout all the world, every single thing has life, so there's nothing that is not part of one mind. They are all there within one mind, and able to function as one. In fact, all things and all lives share the same body, work together as one, and freely give and receive whatever is needed. And yet people still make such a fuss, thinking that they are doing everything by themselves, or that they know better than others.

Living as One Mind

I tell people to live harmoniously, as one mind, because this is the only way forward for us. If you don't uncover your true self, you can't know whether you are acting in accord with one mind or moving in opposition to one mind. To put it another way, if you don't know what you are doing, you won't be able to understand others. If you don't understand others, how can you know the principles of the universe or the essence of the Dharma realm? If you don't know your own foundation, you can't know the foundation of the universe. If you don't know your own foundation, you won't be able to function as one mind, nor will you be able to understand life on other planets. All the same things are there — information gathering and processing, politics, and so on. Everything on this planet is also on other planets.

If we can become one mind and function together harmoniously, then even helping with the development of the universe isn't particularly difficult. "Developing the universe" means providing good seeds of consciousness to other planets and stars, and helping those seeds to flourish. This is development. If those seeds are successful, then that place, too, becomes part of our community. Every single planet, every single star is also myself. So there's no place that isn't my community, there's no behavior that isn't my behavior, and no form of life that isn't my life. I've said this before: The spark of our fundamental mind can burn away all the karma and discriminations of the universe. This is possible because our fundamental mind is endowed with everything. Energy, the ability for everything to communicate, to function automatically, to connect — all these arise from the basic functioning of our foundation.

Some people say that life is pointless because we just get old and die, losing everything in the end. I don't see it like that. Rather, we continue on; it's just our body that we change. People talk about dying, but from the very beginning there was never any unique thing that was "born." When a larva falls from a tree to the ground, it's because it intends to become a cicada. It's not dying; it's changing its shape. It's moving from one form to another, not dying and disappearing.

Earth, water, fire, and air gave rise to microorganisms, and everything else evolved from those. These four elements that formed us didn't suddenly appear out of nothing. They arose from the foundation, and they return there. We were all born because the foundation exists, and we are here now because it exists. There is no living and dying; we're just continuously changing our shapes and moving from here to there. This is always happening every instant, with nothing remaining the same, so how could karma, genetics, causality, or the cycle of rebirth find any place to stick to? We're not actually caught by those things, we're just flowing naturally with the rhythms of the waves. We're just continuously moving from here to there.

Hmm. As I look around, some of you don't seem to understand what I'm talking about. So let me just jump to the conclusion: through spiritual practice, you too can become a Buddha. If you are able to become a true, free person, you can completely change everything in our world, including our future. Without ever moving your body, you could supply the energy to sustain everyone. Everyone has this ability within them. Everyone has this incredible source of energy within them. With this power, it's even possible to draw forth matter and create livable environments in harsh places like Jupiter. For example, you can lay the groundwork for sustaining life by creating more oxygen there.

If we've been consistently relying upon our fundamental mind, not only can we help with the development of the universe, we can also keep our bodies healthy. If some part of our body breaks down, such as our liver or intestines, we can help it recover. In this way, people can live with vitality.

The Power within Us

There is a power that arises from deep and consistent practice, and if this becomes strong enough, we can even bring forth and use the energy from other stars and planets. "Far" and "near" don't exist. Although some place may be many light years away, it's all within the palm of Buddha's hand. It's all right here, because there is nothing that's not also yourself. If we try to reach out to something without going through our fundamental mind, then even though it's right in front of us, it may as well be a thousand miles away. However, if through our fundamental mind we become one with something, then even though it's a thousand or a million miles away, it's as if it were right next to us.

Therefore, at this critical moment, you have to know how to take care of others, as well as our planet. What's the path forward that will allow us to help develop our nation and the world? How can we ensure that there will be enough energy and resources? You need to know that we have within us the power to answer all of these questions. The ability to provide sufficient energy and other resources is within us. As you practice relying upon your fundamental mind, how to take care of all these things will become clear to you.

In the old days, you had to use your body to protect the nation and to do things like politics or commerce. Now, all of those things can be done without moving your body. You can become one with other people, and other people can become one with you, because mind has no form and nothing to grasp. In ancient times, this ability was called the power of manifestation. For example, in order to lead the country in a positive direction, I can also become one with the defense minister. If I become one with a politician, then it's as if I'm lending them my wisdom and spiritual ability so that they can do good for the country.

Similarly, the time has passed when we can choose people for such positions based upon their appearance, their background, or how well they give speeches. Instead, we have to be able to know their minds. We have to know how, through our fundamental mind, to become one with people and function together with them.

A person involved in politics needs to be aware of the unseen aspect that underlies politics. Could this be called something like a god? No, not really. It's not this and it's not that. Yet, it's there in the middle of everything. It's this fundamental mind that can embrace and take care of anything in the entire universe. It can bring in and send out anything through the sense organs, and if you've awakened to this mind, you can become one with politicians and act through them. There's nothing that's not myself — there's no pain that's not my pain, no circumstances that aren't my circumstances, no words that aren't my words. So how could you not become one with someone? Because of this, we can change the direction of our society, we can ensure upright development, and we can ensure that our culture blossoms and is harmonious.

For example, there are insects and parasites that harm plants and animals, right? Through your fundamental mind, you can gather their consciousnesses all together and help them evolve. If you can do this, then you can use this method to embrace everything. There's no one and nothing that you need to throw away. Otherwise, you'll have to chase after so many things, trying to get rid of them one by one. There are just too many things to deal with them like that.

Deepening Yourself

If you would improve the level you're living at, take all of those things that you would throw away or exclude, and entrust them all to the great furnace within you. There, they will all be melted down, and will come back out as something good. You'll never be able to raise your level by manipulating the material world, or through scholarly knowledge or cleverness. Take all the things you know, and all that you've learned, and dump them entirely into this furnace; then, your true self will come alive, and your level will change.

What I'm saying is that your life right now, just as it is, should be meditation, and meditation in action. So live while taking everything that comes up in your life and completely letting go of it to this furnace. Don't give yourself a headache by searching around outside of yourself, chasing after famous practitioners, looking for holy relics to worship, or searching for "special" places to practice.

What's the origin of everything? It all arises from our true self. This true self perceives and responds to everything through our sense organs. It's the one that does everything, the one that has been leading us and taking care of us for untold billions of years. Now that you know what it does, trust that it will take care of you. Living like this is the essence of meditation, and if you keep doing this, that which you're seeking will be revealed.

If you have to meditate by sitting down and crossing your legs, then as soon as you stand up, your meditation is over. How could that truly be called Seon(Zen)? Sitting meditation and other kinds of physical training may be useful sometimes, and if you train your body hard enough, or sit long enough, your thoughts will calm down and you'll feel a sense of peace. But that's not enough. That can never lead you to the great meaning. Those kinds of practices can never help you penetrate the silver mountains and iron walls.

Go forward entrusting everything to your foundation, without missing a single thing. Know that although everything enters and leaves you, there's no place for even the tiniest piece of gunk to stick to. Don't let anything trip you up, including what you hear from inside. If you think it's acceptable to steal others' property because it seemed like your true self said so, well, that's just nonsense. Anyone born as a human being has at least a basic sense of good judgment, fairness, and propriety. So it's not necessary for me to say more about things like this, things that are so far outside the realm of common sense.

People who are serious about spiritual practice need to throw everything into this furnace that is our fundamental mind, including all ideas of Buddhism, Christianity, Islam, and so forth. Melt everything down there; then what arises again from that will be a treasure of this world.

Names and labels are made by dividing things, but is there anything that could exist outside of the truth? No. The ship you are now on isn't some pleasure cruise. You don't even know where it's going. You're just helplessly along for the ride. On this vast ocean, you don't even know where you are, let alone where you've come from. Just following along with things, it never even occurs to you to try to look outside the boat. Not knowing where the boat has come from or where it's going, how could you be so certain in your opinions, insisting that you know so much, criticizing others, and getting into all kinds of arguments?

Let's compare the Earth to your body. The Earth also has organs that function like the stomach, liver, kidneys, and intestines. In order for each part to live, they have to cooperate. They have to work together. But what happens if they are always arguing with each other? If they start laying claim to different areas, and building walls around "mine" and "yours," your body will die! The Earth, too, will die if something like this happens. If one place goes bad, soon everything that depends upon that area will collapse. Yet if minds become one and harmonious, then that collapse can be prevented. And then the direction of our society changes as well. Listen! When you don't even know how to take care of yourself, when you argue with others and close yourself off to them, how could you be able to clearly see, to clearly hear, and to wisely respond to even your family, to say nothing of society, the world, or the universe?

That which is Truly Precious

What is Buddhism? Is it something that teaches you to entrust your precious life to superstitions? Could such a thing be called Buddhism? I know there are some people here who've bought talismans, and keep them in their pillows or walk around with them in their pockets. Stop doing this. You were born to be a precious one — someone who would do something wonderful in this world. Will you waste your time here with useless pieces of paper? Why would you entrust your precious life to those? Relying on things outside yourself like talismans can hardly be a true religion. You need to understand what's truly going on — you need to understand your fundamental mind — and you need to put that understanding into action.

This most precious mind of ours is what allows us to breathe in and out, to move, and to live with vitality. It is Buddha itself. If we entrust a thought to this precious, fundamental mind of ours, it comes back out as the Dharma. If we apply this to the things in our life, it manifests into the world. Usually, when you see Buddhas, Dharma-protecting spirits, doctors, judges, and so on, you're probably seeing these and automatically thinking of them as apart from yourself. However, by entrusting a single thought to your foundation, you can become all of these. Do you only believe in what you can see with your eyes? Really? Inside your body, right now, there are billions of lives that are working unseen on your behalf. They're all serving you. You, the CEO. Do you have any idea how sacred and delightful you are?

The servants that are taking care of your body have even put up defenses around every single cell, protecting each of them from outside intruders. Why are you turning your back on these servants who are ceaselessly protecting you, and instead trying to rely upon others? Why aren't you trying to rely upon your foundation? When you're hurt or sick, it may be necessary to go see a doctor, but become one with that doctor! Your mind has to become one with that doctor, as well as with the beings within you who are ill. Then your body won't be damaged, and even if you have a disease, it won't cause big problems. If you can become one mind and function harmoniously with the lives within you, the disease may even completely disappear.

This applies to every aspect of our lives, at home and in society, as well as illnesses. For example, even if you're writing poetry, you should create living poems that have the power to touch people. Don't be someone who comes up with clever, dead poems. No matter whether you're writing, dancing, or whatever you do, it must be something alive! If it's dead, it's pointless, because it can't deeply connect with people.

Please listen carefully, even though I can't speak eloquently. If I were thinking about trying to come up with sophisticated or clever ways of expressing myself, my words would be useless. They would lack the deep connection with the truth that living words have. They would have no true power to help others. Please understand this principle.

I'm not telling you about these things out of some hope for something for myself, either in this life or next. Even though the energy it costs me to give you deeply true guidance feels like it could be measured in cups of my blood, I don't care. Do you know why? Because we have to face whatever confronts us without fear. Whether you are facing swords, thorns, or fields full of rocks, don't flinch from any of it. Do your best to go forward taking it all as something to practice with. What are you afraid of? Whether you die in your youth or in old age, you'll still have to die once. If you can let go of the fear of dying, there's nothing you cannot do. Nothing can scare you.

And yet, even dying isn't something extraordinary; it is only changing shapes. I can't begin to describe how many times you've died and changed your shape. Even in this very life, you're continuously dying and changing, dying and changing, bit by bit, until, all at once, you change a lot. This is how we're living our lives. The only thing in the middle of all of this that doesn't change is your Juingong, your foundation.

You've probably met people who think that nothing is more important than money. I try to explain to them that money isn't even something we own; we only manage it for a short while.

But they just don't want to hear this. When I tell them that there is something eternal within us that is always working on our behalf, they don't have any idea what I'm talking about. When some people hear that money and property are ours for only a short while, they respond by clinging ever more tightly. Still others respond by just wasting their money, spending it like water. Sigh. People have so many different ways and levels of thinking! You should know, however, that spending money wisely is actually harder than earning it. If you want to have a lot of money, you'd better start by learning how to spend it wisely.

People have gone to jail for even stealing a loaf of bread, haven't they? Could a piece of bread really be worth all that hardship? Yet that decision only took an instant. Just one thought, one decision can completely change our lives. Long ago, Jesus told those who wished to taste his kingdom to come forward, leaving behind all of their possessions. The Buddha, too, said that those who wished to undertake this practice should set aside their attachments to families and possessions.

Do you realize how important raising a good thought can be? Why do you have so much energy wrapped up in objects of desire, thinking they'll be yours forever? How can I even express how wonderful it is when there is no "mine" and "yours"? When everything is complete just as it is? You have to understand that nothing is yours; it all belongs to that which is fundamentally doing everything. Even this body isn't yours. It's functioning because of your true nature, so you have to entrust everything about it to your true nature.

Long ago, *Kyongho*[21] Sunim met some boys gathering firewood in the mountains, and bet them that they couldn't hit him. If they could, he'd give them a few coins. So they swung and hit him, but he shook his head, saying they'd missed. The boys began to cry and stopped trying, feeling like he was cheating them. So Kyongho Sunim held out some coins, "Okay. Here's an advance payment. Keep trying to hit me." This may seem like just a silly story, but it is very much not.

Have you ever heard the expression that if you truly want to learn something, you have to pay for it? You cannot imagine the hardships you've gone through, nor how much *virtue and merit*[22] you've accumulated to reach this point where you are ready and the circumstances are right for you to learn about the practice of relying upon your fundamental mind. So it is my deepest wish that you will take what I've said here today and diligently work at putting it into practice, until you understand this to your very core.

Thank you. Let's stop here for today.

---

21. Kyongho Sunim (鏡虛惺牛, 1846-1912) was the greatest Seon master of his era, and is responsible for much of the current vitality of Korean Buddhism. He had five great disciples, one of whom, Hanam Sunim, was Daehaeng Kun Sunim's teacher. Over fifty percent of the Buddhist monks and nuns in Korea can trace their lineage directly back to him.

22. Virtue and merit (公德): Here this term refers to the results of helping people or beings unconditionally and non-dually, without any thought of self or other. It becomes virtue and merit when you "do without doing," that is, doing something without the thought that "I did such and such." Because it is done unconditionally, all beings benefit from it.

In The Heart Of A Moment

This Dharma talk was given by
Daehaeng Kun Sunim on July 6, 1997.

July 6, 1997

It's a real pleasure to see everyone gathered here together to learn the Dharma. When I visited the U.S. this time, I met many Americans, and again, I felt that their eyes, their attitude, and their whole being was extremely focused on learning about spiritual practice. They were so intent that it seemed like they never took their eyes off me, and absorbed everything I told them.

They were definitely people of a higher spiritual level. It's harder for people at a lower level to sense this underlying essence, but the higher someone's level, the more serious and determined they are to understand this. I was very touched by everyone's deep sincerity. Coming back to Korea, I'm indeed glad to see so many of you here, making such efforts to learn about practice even when the weather is so hot and humid. Although we may speak different languages, our minds are all the same.

Everything is Done by your Fundamental Mind

If you're trying to understand what I'm telling you about our fundamental mind by relying upon academic or theoretical knowledge, a thousand years could pass and still you won't have made any progress, to say nothing of realizing enlightenment. One of the most basic things you need to understand is this: Every movement and function of your body is ultimately being done by your fundamental mind. The consciousnesses of the lives within your body are in charge of all the different parts of your body, and are ensuring that everything functions properly; but it is your foundation, your fundamental mind, that governs these consciousnesses. The energy that these consciousnesses use to respond to the thoughts you give rise to all comes from your fundamental mind. Without the tiniest exception, every single thing you do is possible because of the primordial energy given off by your foundation. Even though our foundation doesn't move, it is what causes everything in the universe to move.

This fundamental mind that we all have is not limited to certain functions, roles, or places. It's utterly boundless. It is this infinite foundation of our mind that has, time after time, allowed us to develop and evolve. It's right and correct for me to say that when we undertake spiritual practice, we need to take the bright light of our fundamental mind as our guide. Yet inherently there is no "bright light," no "fundamental mind," no "door to the truth," and no "crossroads between the visible and the unseen realms." Fundamentally, just as we are, we are all naturally flowing with the truth. All of these terms are just skillful methods used by teachers to help people move forward.

Let's take a look at the way people usually think about things. People usually say that something is good or bad, it's a virtue or a vice, someone is smart or stupid, something is long or short, someone should be blamed or shouldn't be, and so on. Yet all of these distinctions are actually you standing in your own way. Inherently it can't even be said that wrongdoings exist or don't exist. This is so profound and mysterious. Because of the level that human beings are at, which is much higher than other animals, they are able to return things to their fundamental mind. In so doing, in letting go of things such as misconduct, karma, *ignorance*,[23] and so on, those things can no longer be said to exist or not exist.

Letting Go Unconditionally

I'm always telling people that no matter whether they've done something wrong or not, they should just have faith in their fundamental mind and return everything there unconditionally. I say this because when you unconditionally put something into your fundamental mind, it disappears. It happens in this way: When you let go of things without dwelling on them, that message is communicated to all the parts of your body. Through your cerebrum, it is input into the most essential, spiritual part of ourselves, and from there it's communicated to all the parts of the body. If you let go without any attachments to the outcome, without any "it's going well," or "it's going badly," or other discriminations, then the things that were input during a lower level of spirituality will disappear and be replaced by the new input. Because you let go unconditionally, it disappears unconditionally.

---

23. Ignorance (無明)**:** Literally this means darkness. It is the unenlightened mind that does not see the truth. It is being unaware of the inherent oneness of all things, and it is the fundamental cause of birth, aging, sickness, and death.

In this practice, there's no place for making all kinds of discriminations, judgments of right or wrong, or for insisting upon knowing the reasons for all of the things that we encounter. If you get caught up in these things, you won't be able to even glimpse the realm of the dead. Look at a dying person: they're one breath away from having to leave behind their children and loved ones. Do you think they can worry about "why" or demand explanations? No. None of those matter to them now. They just enter the realm of the dead without caring about the reasons.

Likewise, if you would be able to enter the unseen realm and take care of the things there, you have to enter without reasons or explanations. In this realm, when you see, hear, or act, there's no moment of seeing, hearing, or doing. When you become aware of something that needs to be done, you naturally take care of it fully and completely. This is the truth of emptiness that applies to everyone and every place.

However, if you keep insisting on having reasons and explanations, how could you ever experience this unseen realm? If you were dying right now, would you really feel like arguing over the best way to do things? Dying people just leave. Even the Buddha said, "I came from the Way and I return to the Way." And it's the same for each of us. If I could add to this, I would say, "We all came from the Way, our life is the Way, and we all return to the Way."

As we've lived through life after life, everything we've done while caught up in our bad *habits*,[24] clinging, and desires has

---

24. Habits (習): These include not just the ways of thought and behavior learned in this life, but also all of those tendencies of thought and behavior that have accumulated over endless eons.

left behind a residue that covers our mind. This in turn causes all kinds of bothersome thoughts to arise. In today's society, life is so busy, and there are so many stressful things; wouldn't it be nice if we could just let go of those as they arise, and go forward at ease? Don't get caught up in trying to figure out the reasons for all the bothersome things that confront you. If you just let go of them one by one as they arise, then your foundation can absorb them all.

Let your foundation absorb everything that comes from the six senses; let it absorb the *Noble Eightfold Path*,[25] and let it absorb the *Six Paramitas*.[26] Let go of all those things to your foundation, so that it can absorb them, and go forward accepting everything you encounter as if it were a Buddha giving you a teaching. Treat everything equally. Make your mind a home where Buddhas and Bodhisattvas reside together with all beings. We are going forward as practitioners of the Dharma for the sake of tasting this place.

Rhetorical or theoretical arguments are unnecessary. Arguing over or insisting upon understanding every single point is utterly useless – it's endless, and never takes you anywhere. People try to use their intellect to manage their life, but it is your thoughts entrusted to your foundation, which then work through the unseen realm, that can truly take care of things.

---

25. Noble Eightfold Path (八正道)**:** Correct view, correct thought, correct speech, correct action, correct livelihood, correct effort, correct mindfulness, and correct concentration. Living in accord with these will lead one to enlightenment and make it possible to free other beings as well.

26. Six Paramitas (六波羅蜜)**:** Charity, morality, restraint, effort, meditation, and wisdom. These are the six practices of a Bodhisattva, and when applied with a selfless attitude, will help free ordinary beings as well.

Although I use the word "thought," that's still just a method to point you in the right direction. When I saw this water [holding up a cup], I just picked up the cup and took a drink, without anything we'd normally call a thought. I just drank it. We're able to do everything in our lives like this, but we often can't because we get caught up in ideas such as, "I can't do this," "I don't know how," "I have too much bad karma," "I must have done many terrible things in the past to be suffering like this," and so on.

However, just leap over all of these things and take care of those problems through your mind. Your mind is faster than the speed of light, and when it runs here and there, its feet don't touch the ground! It can do things in an instant, and unlike ordinary light, nothing can block the light of mind.

The Urgent Need to be Able to Use Our Inherent Abilities

You really need to understand the ability of mind. For example, if there is a problem with the ozone layer, many other problems would result, wouldn't they? This would contribute towards the melting of glacial and polar ice, which in turn would lead to so many floods and fires that people wouldn't be able to continue living in those areas. So if you want to fix that hole in the ozone, there is a way you can go and repair it without even moving your body. If you are very resolute, if you are very determined that you must do something about this, then you can go there directly. You can go there, but not with your body; that remains here. You can go and take care of the problem before it becomes worse. As a result, the hole won't let in as much solar radiation, and even though some problems will still happen, the hole will gradually become smaller. In this way, you can help prevent the ice from melting, as well as the other related problems.

This ability to use our minds also relates to another truth of this world. Let's compare the Earth to a house we live in. Imagine what life would be like if it's a small house and there are too many people living there. What's eventually going to happen if it's so crowded that people can't even find a place to lie down and sleep?

To grow crops like lettuce and cabbage, we start by spreading seeds all across the ground. However, when they sprout, the plants are often too close to each other. In this case, none of them will be able to grow well. So they are thinned out, with some of the plants pulled up and space created between the remaining ones. As the plants grow bigger, they have to be thinned several more times, with more and more of the plants pulled up.

This process of thinning can even be called a law of nature. Take the example of pepper plants: even in the case of big healthy plants, when two are growing right next to each other, one has to be pulled up so that the other can flourish. Otherwise, neither of them would produce anything useful. Regardless of whether things are big or small, if there are too many crowded into one area, they still need to be thinned in order for them to flourish. This applies to every kind of life in the world, and, if we look around, we can see that more and more are being thinned. The process of thinning is on the increase. However, if we can deepen our spiritual ability, we can help ease the suffering caused by this process.

Further, if there are many people who can harmoniously take care of both the material realm and the spiritual realm while maintaining the balance between these two, then this world will change from the middle realm to a higher realm, a realm of Buddhas and Bodhisattvas. At that point, another planet can become the middle realm, and perform the duties of the middle realm. If this world becomes an upper realm, then all of the things that we no longer need will all move there and create a new middle realm. I'm not talking about people loading things up and carrying them from one place to another.

Please Keep Relying Upon Your Fundamental Mind

The workings of these secret principles probably seem hard to understand and hard to accept, but this is how things are. That's why I've spoken of plants and thinning, and how the things we no longer need will appear somewhere else. Something terrible is happening to human beings, and the same thing is happening to animals and even microorganisms. However, if there are many people who know how to rely upon their fundamental mind, then everything can be changed. All of this will depend upon how diligently we have been practicing and to what extent we've raised our spiritual level. It's critical that everyone realizes this.

If we can raise our level like this, we'll become aware of the amazing rights and power of our fundamental mind. Figuratively speaking, it's like flowers blooming in the air and then bearing fruit. Even though we are all endowed with such tremendous rights and ability, do you realize how many people have never thought about this even once, and are just slowly passing the time until they die? So I hope that all of you will continue to diligently rely upon your fundamental mind until the very last day of your life. Then you will be able to come back to this world with a higher spiritual level and a deeper understanding of the workings of our fundamental mind. Sakyamuni Buddha, too, came into this world like that. He was born fully understanding our fundamental mind, but in order to help guide people, he went through the whole process of life and spiritual practice.

How well the things in our lives go depends upon how thoroughly we are letting go of them to our foundation. Because we live in this middle realm, the things we do become karma and suffering. Shouldn't we be at least trying to ensure that we're creating good karma, and not increasing suffering? This is also the path. This way is the path; that way is the path; there's no way that isn't the path. The truth is within everything, so there's no point in getting caught up in thinking that things turned out well or badly. Don't waste your mental energy in arguments over right and wrong. Instead, today, work on trying to ask the questions that are deeply fundamental to you, so that we can have a helpful and meaningful discussion.

If I keep talking about things you're unclear on, my words won't do you any good. So ask me about the parts you don't understand, so that you'll be able to put what I've said into practice. If you don't have the experiences that result from putting your understanding into practice, then even though I tell you more things about the world, the universe, and what's truly possible, you won't understand me. Just listening to me is utterly different from actively applying what I've said to the problems you face.

Ask questions until you completely understand what I'm talking about. You really need to be able to put this into practice. Everyone in the world is living together under the same roof, called the Earth. If part of our house is damaged, everyone living there will be harmed. So, practice and protect your home. You're the one living there, so you're the one who has to do this.

When I was in the U.S., several newspapers reported on an incident where there were both male and female gang members in a school, and that they fought and even killed each other. The details were so vicious. Seeing this, I realized that we all have to get a grip on ourselves. We all need to be centered and alert. Otherwise.... This is why, today, I'm telling you about all these things.

The truth existed before Sakyamuni Buddha was born. He studied the truth and taught everyone how things really are, yet, in spite of this, people spend their time talking about useless things. If you keep doing this, you'll die with the same the level you were born with. You won't have evolved at all. The seed of your next life won't have changed. Unless you make up your mind to change, life after life you'll be reborn at the same level. If you just pass the time until you get sick and die, you'll be reborn at exactly that same level. Yet, your fundamental mind is inherently endowed with such incredible and profound ability. So if you want to evolve, take all of your habits, attachments, and desires, and let go of them to your fundamental mind. There, they will all be dissolved. This is the process of erasing old input, and making change possible.

You really need to understand what I'm saying. Even if Sakyamuni Buddha were right here beside you, you're still the one who has to do the work necessary to become enlightened.

He can't do it for you. Even Sakyamuni Buddha can't breathe for you, eat for you, be sick instead of you, or go to the toilet for you. You're the only one who can do those things. In a way, our life is truly lonely and solitary. "But I have a family," you may be thinking; yet even your cherished family is composed of solitary individuals. You're the one who has to do this, so learn to rely upon your fundamental mind. Don't finish your life as a tiny radish! You've all seen those, right? All leaf and no root. Useless. Don't keep repeating such a life over and over. Become a giant, tasty radish that can feed all kinds of people! So if you have questions, ask! Try to ask about the basic things you need help putting into practice.

Questioner 1(male): Sunim, I'm glad to see you. Recently, our country has been going through a lot of economic problems. "Voluntary retirement" and "early retirement" are on everyone's lips. The number of unemployed keeps increasing, and a lot of people are suffering because of the economy. I was one of those people who experienced many difficult things, and I'm here today to share my experiences with others. I hope that my story will give some comfort and hope to others, and I would also like to ask for your guidance about some parts I'm still struggling with.

Last February I sold the company I'd run for ten years. Afterward, I developed a detailed plan for another business that I intended to start. I took all of the money I'd received from the sale of my old company and used it to get everything set up for the new company. However, something completely unexpected happened, and all my plans collapsed. I lost most of my money, and realized that I had no idea what I was going to do. I began to panic a bit, and realized that I needed to plan for the future. I took a hard look at our household expenses, but there was almost nothing that could be cut. My oldest daughter had just started college, and if I was ever going to get anything started again, I had to maintain my social status, and keep up with my social obligations. [In Korea, among other things, this means lots of wedding gifts, birthday gifts, dinners, and so forth.] I thought about taking a job driving people home after they've had too much to drink, or finding a job as a day laborer, but our situation was deteriorating to the extent that those kinds of jobs wouldn't help.

Things went on like this for a while, and no matter where I looked, there was no hope in sight. All of my prospects seemed as dark as night. I had no idea what I could do to support my family. I became restless and depressed, and for a week I didn't even leave my home. It was like I was living in prison. However, the choir at the Seon Center met once a week, and I worked up enough energy to attend rehearsals. That night, the choir director emphasized the importance of having an open heart and singing with a cheerful voice, so rehearsal was a very liberating experience, and all my distracting thoughts went away.

I'd spent a week feeling extremely frustrated and overwhelmed, when a thought suddenly arose, "What a waste of time! I'm studying under a great Seon master – what am I doing acting like this?" I reflected upon myself and realized I had been completely absorbed in possibilities for future work and business, and had spent all my energy focused on outer things. I realized that I'd been doing everything backwards, and, sink or swim, I had to observe my own mind.

As soon as this occurred to me, I began to watch. At first I was bursting with anxiety and unable to rest. However, thanks to this spiritual practice, I began to feel tranquil and untroubled within just a few days. Because I felt comfortable, I began to feel like leaving the house, and was able to go out and visit friends and business acquaintances.

In the course of this, I discovered an unexpected opportunity to start a new business. Everything I'd planned for earlier was gone, so I just grabbed that opportunity without getting caught up in worrying about whether it would succeed or not. Strangely enough, things turned out so well that it was as if that business had been waiting for me the whole time. The business I had put so much planning into had slipped through my fingers, but when I threw myself into the business that came to me accidentally, it seemed like help and opportunities came from all directions. It felt as though some mysterious, unseen hand was helping me. This new business did so well that before long I was earning as much as before. Everything I'd been worried about has disappeared. By the way, all of this happened over just three or four months. I hope that my experience can give some hope and encouragement to others who are suffering economic hardships.

Previously, I'd always thought of something like the "realm of the dead" as some state where we have lost our body. Yet now I've begun to feel that I'm truly in the realm of the living only when I've let go of "me" and "I." When I'm full of thoughts of "I," I now feel like I'm wandering in the realm of the dead. Also, it feels like the core of spiritual practice is first of all to quietly and peacefully observe our mind without getting caught up in things happening outside of ourselves, and then to respond peacefully to what comes up. If we don't want to do something, then that's fine too. Is there any other way to undertake spiritual practice? I would like to ask you for a teaching on this matter.

Kun Sunim: There is no other way. To go back to your earlier story, it's like you messed up the first button on your shirt, so all of the buttons afterwards were misaligned. However, you realized you'd made a mistake, so you went back to the first button, started over, and got things straightened out. No matter what kind of problem confronts you, don't let it worry you. Even if the entire world collapses, don't flinch. If you keep practicing as you've described, then it probably won't be necessary for you to go around trying to borrow money, either. Everyone can live freely and naturally like this. Nonetheless, people fill their lives with pain and unnecessary complications. So live while letting go of everything to your foundation. You have to die in order to truly see yourself. However, I'm not talking about the death of your body.

You have to know what it means to die while alive. People call dying with the body "nirvana," but this isn't true nirvana. For true nirvana, you have to die while alive. Everything that's ever been and ever will be is ceaselessly changing and functioning together as one whole. When you can live in accord with this, your life will be so smooth and restful! Instead of shallow love, utterly deep compassion will well up within you, and fill everything you do, whether it's at home with your family or with people you've just met. Thus, shouldn't you be practicing such that all your actions, thoughts, and words can truly have the power to help people? If you give something and brag about it, or make an offering hoping to trick the universe into giving you something, how could those kinds of offerings give rise to any true benefit? When you give offerings because of greed, all sorts of malicious problems will follow the trail of that greedy residue back to you. These kinds of problems happen so often to people.

So "live comfortably" doesn't mean just relaxing your body or feeling at ease. It means while putting your mind at ease, if there's something you have to take care of by moving your body, you get up and do it. In this way your life becomes more healthy and balanced, and you'll come to know the meaning of "doing without doing." Then, even though you're active, no traces of "I" or "me" will be left behind. The body may leave footsteps, but there should be no footsteps left behind mind.

You spoke for a long time, but your experiences and questions will provide others with a good outline of practice. Thank you.

Questioner 1: I'd like to ask something else. I heard there is someone who grows crops in a greenhouse, and plays recordings of your Dharma talks for the plants. Apparently the plants in that greenhouse grow faster and produce more. This seems to me a quite natural result. As you've said, there is energy in sound waves, and so the energy of your recording is transmitted to the plants. I suspect that the sound waves of your talks are a spiritual energy that's manifesting into the material realm, and so the plants are able to grow better. Although I'm not as spiritually realized as you, how can I, too, send forth this kind of spiritual energy into the world? How can we infuse this energy into the things we do and make?

Kun Sunim: Your question is related to something I've wanted to talk about today: If you're working on relying upon your fundamental mind, when you entrust a thought or need, and follow it up with the necessary action, then energy will naturally arise from those things. I've said before that our mind, the entire universe, and all life are connected through our foundation, haven't I? Because of the law of emptiness – this interpenetrated, ceaselessly changing nature – the energy generated by your practice, thoughts, and actions can spread out to everything. To use the example of the problems in American schools, if, deep down inside, many people begin to think, "Oh, this has to change," then it really does start to change. Those kinds of problems happen when people aren't aware of the spiritual realm or how it functions. All of their energy is devoted to blindly charging after aspects of the material realm. However, the energy from our practice reaches out everywhere. If through this we can give others a sense of this energy that arises from our fundamental mind, wouldn't this world become a different place?

Not only human beings can feel this energy. Animals, plants, and even microbes can all feel it. So you shouldn't be content to use your practice for improving just your own life. You have to also use it to help others live better. While doing this, when some wisdom or understanding occurs, take that and see where else it might apply to. See what else you can incorporate that wisdom or understanding into. You'll find that the energy of emptiness can be applied to every field of study and existence.

Questioner 1: Thank you. From now on, I'll let go of all ideas that "I've" done something. I'll ceaselessly continue forward on the path of knowing my true self. Thank you again.

Kun Sunim: Good. Just remember that throwing away "I" doesn't mean throwing away your daily life or deserting the people around you. Rather, it is the opportunity to experience a truly special love and compassion for them.

Questioner 2(male): I have to say that when I think of how hard you work so that others may brighten their spirit, I feel a bit ashamed of myself. I'd like to ask you about gratitude and the idea of giving something back.

I always feel grateful when things work out well after I've overcome some difficulty. I would entrust to my foundation the gratitude I felt toward the Buddha or you, Kun Sunim, or other sunims, but it felt like something was missing. I wondered why I felt that way. I finally realized that I wasn't giving any credit to my true self. My true self is the source of everything that's happened to me, and is what has ultimately caused things to work out well. However, I wasn't seeing this at all, and instead gave all the credit to Buddhas and sunims. One day, it suddenly occurred to me that, "All of those good things have happened because of my true self. So I need to feel grateful to my true self, and entrust it with even that feeling. Then everything will work harmoniously, as one." Is this idea correct?

Kun Sunim: You've come to the right conclusion. Really. Look, after defecating, you yourself wipe your rear end. If you want to give gratitude to someone for that, it should be to yourself, right? Why should sunims be involved in that? If a practitioner keeps calling out, "Buddha! Buddha!" he or she will lose sight of themselves. If the Buddha goes to the toilet, will that relieve the pressure in your bowels?

What you are talking about also applies to ideas such as "giving back" or "returning merit." Taking care of your rear end after going to the toilet is giving back, and your body digesting a meal is also giving back. It's the same for both big and small things. Cleaning up after work, repaying your debts, saying "thanks" when finished – all of these are forms of giving back, or returning the merit.

Further, when you hold a memorial service for your parents, you should be directing your gratitude for your parents' love and kindness to your Juingong. For it is through Juingong that you are able to repay everything that your parents and ancestors have done for you. Return everything there. Everything, including the spirits of your deceased family members, is all together with your Juingong. Even though the very air around us is filled with an infinite variety of spirits, they are all one. They are all of one kind. So by returning your sincerity and gratitude to that one place, absolutely everyone is included. You said that you always felt grateful to sunims, but their Juingong and your Juingong are not separate. So when you express your deep gratitude to Juingong, you are also expressing it to everyone, including sunims. All Buddhas and Bodhisattvas are also there in Juingong. "Returning merit" and "giving back" are also the same as this.

Questioner 2: When I started feeling grateful to my true self, I was surprised at how grateful I also felt towards sunims.

I'd like to ask you about something else: when a friend is sick at home or in the hospital, I used to wonder whether it was necessary to visit them in person. I found myself wondering, "couldn't I just encourage them through mind?" Lately though, I often find that I'd rather have a nice visit with them, chatting and just being there with an open heart. I'm still not sure which way is correct.

Kun Sunim: In your life, the spiritual realm and the material realm need to be balanced. If you were to put them on a scale, it shouldn't be tilted to one side or the other. When you go visit your friends, your mind and their mind meet, and energy goes back and forth, brightening both sides. In most cases, you have to go in person in order for your friend to know that you were there and for that energy to arise. However, if your friend has awakened, if he or she is someone who can go and come back without moving their body, then even though they are sick, you won't need to go visit them with your body. But if this isn't the case, then you have to go in person in order to help their mind and your mind to connect. You can't ignore the material realm. Without your body, you can't engage in spiritual cultivation. Your body is so precious. It was the unseen realm that gave rise to your body; they aren't separate. They always work together. Your physical body arose from the unseen realm, and it is your Juingong that, through the unseen spiritual realm, leads and guides your body. So, if you truly realize that your body and Juingong work together as one, then as the kids say, "Wow!"

People enshrine a statue of the Buddha in their house, and view Buddha as someone or something much more precious and magnificent than themselves. However, you shouldn't enshrine a Buddha outside of yourself. Buddha is something you enshrine within your own mind. It's something you carry around with you at all times. In ancient days, the great master *Wonhyo*[27] said, "You have to put Buddha under your skin and go forth. Why are you carrying around a Buddha outside of yourself?" Buddha statues were created as a way to help lead people forward, to guide them out of their normal ways of thinking. Bowing is also a good method for becoming humble. There are actually so many ways to help people move forward.

Questioner 2: Thank you.

Kun Sunim: Ah, it seems like everyone is doing well in their spiritual practice. I think everyone here will be able to realize the highest truths of mind.

---

27. Wonhyo Sunim (元曉, 617-686): A Silla dynasty monk who is considered one of Korea's greatest monks. Known for the depth of his enlightenment and penetrating wisdom, Wonhyo wrote numerous commentaries on the sutras, emphasizing that the different teachings of the various schools and sutras were merely different aspects of the same fundamental reality. All were based on the same underlying truth, and the variations were just reflections of the differences between eras, cultures, and people's ability to understand.

Questioner 3(male): Kun Sunim, thank you very much for teaching us today, even though you must be tired after your trip to America. In your Dharma talks, you've told us to let go of both sides, and I think this means to let go of things arising from the visible realm, and things arising from the invisible realm. So whenever I face problems of either type, I work to let go of them. However, it feels like the problems arising from the material realm are more severe. There's one such problem that's been beating me down for the last two years. I've faced it head on, and done my best to keep letting go of it, but it still isn't resolved. That said, I'm not taking even a single step backwards. Even if it kills me, I'll go down facing this head on. It seems that in order to let go of both sides and go forward, the key is to let go of even our concerns for life itself. Is this correct?

The second thing I'd like to ask you is this: When I entrust things to my fundamental mind, sometimes they are resolved quickly, and sometimes they take longer, one or two years. In these cases, do we keep focusing on the problem as if it were a *hwadu*(koan),[28] or do we just let go and entrust it every time we become aware of it?

Kun Sunim: The one who is observing the problem and the one who solves the problem are not separate. In fact, if you've truly experienced this, you'll realize that there's nothing to observe.

---

28. Hwadu (話頭, C. –hua-tou, J. –koan): Traditionally, the key phrase of an episode from the life of an ancient master, which was used for awakening practitioners, and which could not be understood intellectually. This developed into a formal training system using several hundred of the traditional 1,700 koans. However, hwadus are also fundamental questions arising from inside that we have to resolve. It has been said that our life itself is the very first hwadu that we must solve.

Further, the spiritual realm and the material realm always function together as one, so why are you trying to treat them as if they were separate? What I'm saying is that you should just let go of everything to your fundamental mind as it confronts you. When you completely entrust it there, your fundamental mind responds accordingly. When we need rice, we put dried rice into the cooker and then wait. In due time, it comes out soft and ready to eat. Likewise, when we entrust something into the spiritual realm, i.e. our fundamental mind, what was entrusted changes and comes back out into the material realm.

Questioner 3: I see. A problem I'm having is that when it's an issue of illness, of myself or someone close to me, I'll entrust it to Juingong and everything will work out fine. However, when it's a large problem that's entangled in the material realms with something like money, it just seems to go on and on. I'm having a hard time because of problems like these.

Kun Sunim: Don't think like that. Even if it is some problem of the material realm, even if you're about to die, no matter what you're going through, "you" are not the one who is taking care of this. Your foundation, Juingong, gave rise to you, and even now is animating you. So why are you getting caught up in so many useless worries about things. Your life is in the hands of Juingong, which is not separate from you.

Questioner 3: So entrusting even life and death, and then going forward, is the correct method?

Kun Sunim: Yes, it is.

Questioner 3: Thank you.

Kun Sunim: If you truly come to understand that everything functions as one, continuously changing whole, then you can free yourself from all kinds of wearisome hardships and anxieties. It's odd how this works. In many cases the one who is obsessed with living dies, while the one who has no fear of death lives. Do you know why the only son often dies too soon? Because the family dotes excessively on the child. They worry so much about him that it actually becomes a malign influence.

Questioner 4(male): Kun Sunim, how are you? I just finished my mandatory military service and have found a good job. I'd like to settle down and get married, but every time I look in the mirror, it seems like I've lost more hair. I'm kind of worried that this will hurt my chances! So I'm entrusting this to Juingong, hoping my hair will grow back. What do you think about this? [Everyone laughs.]

Kun Sunim: This is why I'm always telling people that Juingong is doing every single thing, so be sure to let go of everything to it. It's impossible for me to address every possible situation, so I've explained it in general terms. Entrust your problem to your Juingong, knowing that "Juingong, if my hair falls out, it will be harder for me to get married. You're the one who has to stop this hair loss." Whenever you're worried about your hair falling out, just let go of that worry to Juingong. And you may even find your hair becoming thicker!

Questioner 4: Thank you so much! I'll be sure to practice like that!

Kun Sunim: [laughs.] That's good, but don't forget there's more. You all have the fundamental energy that can take care of everyone and every place. You can use this energy as much as you want to. If you need a little, you can use a little, and if you need a lot, you can use a lot. You can use it according to the place, the era, and the realm it's needed in. So don't worry about us running out of energy. The very spaces around us are overflowing with energy, and your foundation is connected to all of it. If you understand this principle, then even though you aren't carrying anything around with you, you can freely use this energy whenever you want or need to.

In fact, if you truly understand that you have this fundamental energy that you're endowed with, you can live in any way you wish. You can extend the span of your life, or you can trade your body in for a new, fashionable one! And when your body becomes worn out, it will occur to you that it's time for a new one. However, don't try to visualize a particular type of body or shape, for if you can fully use your inherent abilities to help change the world, you won't be able to imagine the shape or form you will have in the higher realms. The higher your spiritual level, the more likely your shape will be something different from what you expected. So don't try to visualize being reborn with this shape or looking like that. When you die, if you have a particular fixed idea like that, then your shape will tend to be pushed towards that form. Please think about this.

Settle down and get serious about understanding and experimenting with how your fundamental mind works and how it manifests into the material realm. Here at the Seon Center we have a research group, but each one of you is also a researcher. This research is thinking about and examining the phenomena of our daily life, our society, and the universe in which we live. This kind of research isn't the domain of just certain, special people; it's what we all have to do.

Today I happened to see a bit of someone giving a talk on television, and found what they were saying really annoying. If they don't know about this principle of one mind, then no matter how long someone goes on like that, nothing they say will be useful to others, and they'll never make even the tiniest bit of progress. Only through one mind can we heal and dissolve all the things that are troubling us. For me, when someone goes on with such useless stuff, I really can't hear them at all. It's as if nothing is going in my ears. I won't say any more about this, because my criticism might encourage negative ways of thinking that aren't helpful to you.

You should all firmly settle your minds, and develop the ability to make small things into big things, and to make big things into small things. Having the ability to freely take care of things, regardless of whether they are big or small, is what we can attain through this practice of learning to rely upon and use our fundamental mind.

Let me express the truth in a very basic sense: Falling into muck and filthy water is the path, and freeing yourself from muck and dirty water is also the path. The way is found in every single thing you meet. Nothing is excluded. When you completely let go of both "throwing away" and "nothing to throw away," you will attain the ability to freely take care of anything that arises.

Now it's up to you to apply this truth to the things in your life. In this way, you'll come to understand everything for yourself. If you go ahead and put what I've said into practice, you'll naturally come to understand all of this.

One With The Universe

This Dharma talk was given by
Daehaeng Kun Sunim on November 3, 1996.

November 3, 1996

To Save All Beings

I'd like to thank everyone for working so hard to make the Dharma talk at the Olympic Stadium in Seoul such a success. I've been away overseas, so I'm late saying this; nonetheless, thank you. Words fail to express how grateful I feel to you.

I suspect that some of you still haven't recovered yet. You dragged yourselves here through force of will alone. This consciousness we have is so important; without it our body is just a corpse. Shortly after the Seoul Dharma talk, I went to Germany to give a series of talks, and then went straight to Canada for the opening of the new Toronto center. I was so tired I didn't know what country I was in! After returning to Korea, I woke up during the night and couldn't even find the door in my own room! I laughed after I'd woken up a bit – without this mind of ours, the body just stumbles around like a robot.

If you understand this, then you probably have a good idea why I've opened so many branches, and why I'm always imploring you to discover this fundamental mind of yours, what I sometimes call Juingong. If humanity is going to survive, both living beings as well as the dead need to become one mind and work together to preserve the Earth.

I've gone around opening centers all over the world in order to help free the consciousnesses that are trapped in that region. There are often many who died in wars and disasters, who, at the moment of their death, became stuck in that place. Thus, we work to open the door for them to become one mind. Likewise, there are many living people who are similarly stuck in their thoughts, and who can become free by becoming one mind. Although it's not easy to do, when we set up a center, it becomes one with the functioning of the universe,[29] and is directly connected to everything in it.

Sincere application is the path. Truly and sincerely putting what you know into practice is the Way! Without application, there is no path forward. Knowing isn't enough. Prophets and psychics are called small people because they can only tell you what will happen, but they can't do anything about it. However, here at our Anyang center and in centers around the world, we are working to wake up those who are asleep, and to free those who are trapped. In this way, I hope that everyone here can learn to work together as one mind, and go forward in the world using your practice to help people.

So, when we gather together, I'm always telling you to focus within instead of looking around outside of yourself, for every single thing is already being done by your true nature, your Juingong. If you look at the hills, no matter how far apart, they are all still connected, aren't they? Likewise, you must realize that the material realm and the unseen realm are always functioning as one. They're not separate. Do your consciousness

---

29. This includes all visible realms, as well as unseen realms, and the principles by which they function.

and flesh function apart from each other? No, of course not. It's only for the sake of getting people moving that I say things like "Hurry and leave this hill and go to that hill." Here, this hill is the material realm, and that hill is the unseen or spiritual realm. If you realize the spiritual realm, you will instantly understand how it works together as one with the material realm. So I say to you, hurry up and awaken, and cross over to that hill.

As you practice trying to let your Juingong come forward, everything will begin to communicate through it. However, if you are only looking for and following the material aspects, then you won't be able to communicate or become one mind with everything. Thus, nothing you do will be able to give forth true virtue and merit. If even just the cells of your body become one mind and work together, this will give rise to the virtue and merit that will allow you to fulfill the role of a Bodhisattva.

However, if those cells argue among themselves and each goes its own way, before long the whole will break down. It's the same for companies and organizations. If everyone in a company cooperates and works together harmoniously, it will do well. Yet if everyone is arguing and fighting, it won't have much of a future. Therefore, I think it's essential that there are places dedicated to spiritual practice, where everyone can work on becoming one mind with all Buddhas and the universe, and so be able to sustain and protect the Earth.

If the Earth's air heats up, the pressure will eventually cause holes to form in the weaker parts of the atmosphere. If this happens, ice that has remained frozen for thousands of years will begin to melt too fast, and everything will change. It would be as if our entire world was torn apart. Would we be like ants fleeing a flood, struggling and climbing to find high ground? I'm bringing this up now so that you'll have some idea why I've been traveling so much and giving Dharma talks everywhere.

What I've said today about relying upon your fundamental mind is desperately serious. I'm not joking around. If your idea of spiritual practice is going around visiting temples like a tourist, maybe bowing a few times in this hall or that shrine, then everything you are one with — your body, your family, your nation — will be torn to pieces. It's not an exaggeration to say that everything that exists now will be turned under the earth, so that a new era can start. In the past, the world changed only through floods, fire, wars, and the deaths of uncountable people. But now we can use our minds to change things, without having to go through these kinds of disasters. Everything changes according to how you use your mind.

The Need is Urgent

While visiting Germany recently, I realized that huge numbers of people had died there in religious wars. Even though I was already exhausted, I continued to go from place to place, talking with both the dead who were still trapped by the events of four hundred years ago, and the living that were trapped by their own thoughts. I told them how they could be free, and cracked open the door that had imprisoned them. Among the dead stuck in those places were many nuns and priests who had been tortured to death.

I'll come back to this story in a minute, but first let me talk about something else. Someone asked why, when holding a *cheondo*[30] ceremony we set out a plate of steamed rice cake. It's because while living in this world, the habit of eating becomes so deeply ingrained within us that many people can't set it aside even after they're dead. Because of this idea that they need food to survive, spirits often end up staying very close to their children or relatives. Thus, they cannot move forward on their own path, and in their confused state, they often inadvertently cause harm to their families and descendants.

Many other temples write the names of the deceased on a memorial paper and hang them in the Dharma Hall, but we don't do that here. Instead, we explain the Dharma to the deceased for a hundred days, so that they can move forward. Basically, this is extra time for education, where we are inviting them to see, hear, and experience this truth of one mind.

However, if you write their name on a piece of paper and leave it in the Dharma hall, that can actually hold those spirits there. To put it plainly, they now have to receive permission from the living in order to move forward, on top of the permission they need from the unseen realms. This is why when we have a ceremony for someone who has passed on, we write the memorial paper for them only on that day, and then burn it after the ceremony. If we need to have another ceremony for them

---

30. Cheondo (薦度): This involves helping the consciousness of the dead to move forward on their own path. It can happen that beings become "stuck" in their fears, attachments, and illusions, and so can't move forward. Cheondo often involves a special ceremony, but not necessarily, which in a sense educates the consciousness, and so allows it to move forward at a level that more accurately reflects the level they achieved while alive.

later, then we write a new memorial paper for them at that time. Everyone should think deeply about why we do this.

In cases where families don't have the money for the traditional one hundred day ceremony, we tell them to hold just the forty-ninth day ceremony, and we take care of all the necessary education in that time. Also, when families are poor, I'll sometimes direct the deceased to various jobs and assignments that can help them be reborn in this world as a great being, as someone who can truly practice. As they use their practice to help others, the light of that also helps everyone who has karmic affinity with them, including their family from their past life. In this way their children's generation becomes brighter, along with each successive generation. Ha! When I say "great being," you think of someone who wears the gray clothes of a Buddhist monk or nun, don't you? But these aren't required for someone to be a great being.

Following the path of the Bodhisattvas means not harming others in the slightest. But more than that, it means that what you do to others must only benefit them. Otherwise, it will be impossible for you to fulfill the role of a Bodhisattva. Why? Because the universe won't give you its approval, and so it also won't give you its authority, which is necessary to truly fulfill the role of a Bodhisattva. The actions of a Bodhisattva aren't something you can do just because you want to. When we can truly run errands on behalf of the whole, then we can open the door for all of our ancestors, and open their eyes and ears. We can communicate as one with everything in everyplace we visit, and so can free the spirits of the dead who are trapped in those places. We can wake them up from the thoughts they're trapped in, allowing them to go forward on their own path.

A German Nun's Story

When I went to Germany and was staying at our center there, the spirit of a nun abruptly appeared before me. She started talking at length about some historical event that I'd never heard of. There are actually lots of things I don't know about, but if I encounter them and need to know about them, then they become clear to me. Anyway, I just listened for a while, and then asked who she was. She answered, "I lived here about three hundred and fifty years ago." So I changed direction and asked her why she'd come to visit me. She told me the following story:

"At the time I lived here, there was a huge religious war that killed nearly half the people in the land. So many people were sick, starving, or injured in those days that we nuns, who ran the chapel that used to be here, set up three large nursing camps. We raised awnings to shelter people from the sun and rain, and we cared for the sick and dying as best we could. However, in the end many people came and abused us horribly. They killed us, and we were buried on this spot. Many others were also tortured and killed here, and buried with us. From that time until now, we haven't been able to leave this place. Since you've come here, can you help us leave? Can you open the door for us?"

"Oh my dear," I replied, "you've got it backwards. In both Catholic and Buddhist teachings, everyone is interconnected. No one is separate from anyone else, so why would you need me to open the door for you?" I then explained at length to her about this one mind that connects us all.

After hearing this, she ran to the Dharma Hall, bowed three times, and then threw her nun's robes over the garden wall. [Next to the Dharma Hall there is a large area of grass and garden that is enclosed by a concrete wall.]

While we need to understand why spirits get stuck like this and can't move forward, it's also important to be able to free them as a group. A long time ago, I saw that at military cemeteries there were many spirits stuck there, unable to move forward. I realized that I needed to be able to gather them all together and free them so that they could each go forward on their own path. To this end, I practiced doing this at cemeteries, and especially at military cemeteries both in Korea and overseas. We need to be able to save all beings, even those who don't realize they are stuck. It would not be in accord with the Buddha's teachings to think of only those beings who come to you looking for help.

If you save one body, you instantly save all of the beings within it. It's like this. Your ability to set all those spirits free depends upon your ability to rely upon your own fundamental mind, and through that, to become one with everything. Spirits appear because they know who can help them. Those spirits aren't walking to you, or taking steps one at a time. They appear instantly, because mind moves instantly.

WHAT YOU ENTRUST CAN MOVE THE WORLD

Please don't treat this fundamental mind of ours as if it was something you could ignore, or something that's not particularly relevant to you. No matter what, you must practice gathering everything together in your fundamental mind, until even a small, quiet thought entrusted there can come back out and move the entire world. This is why I keep teaching and imploring you to learn to rely upon your fundamental mind.

Currently, all over the world, pollution is becoming worse than ever before. I don't know the proper scientific terms for these things, but if the pollution worsens, the atmosphere will heat up and holes will form in the layers that protect the atmosphere. This would open the way for enormous calamities to happen, including major flooding. Even now pollution is causing serious problems. If it continues, we'll have to completely start our lives over again from nothing. Garbage and such isn't the only source of pollution. For example, in the Alps they've planted great steel pillars for cable cars, and these, too, are a form of pollution.

Skilled doctors will cut away only the damaged parts. But would you want to go under the knife of a doctor who never went to medical school and doesn't even know anatomy? Now we have people who can't tell the difference between a vein and an artery cutting into mountains and planting steel pillars every which way. How could this not be pollution? Can you imagine the damage being done by people who think they're doctors, but who can't even tell left from right?

However, even that damage, that pollution, can be prevented if we use our minds wisely. It is also our minds that can reconnect those cells that have been cut off. The ability of this fundamental mind of ours is so vast and incredible; it can truly do anything.

Within our bodies, the intestines, colon, and other organs communicate and work with each other to enable us to live. The Earth is also like this, and has a channel connecting the North Pole with the South Pole, and a channel that works to process and excrete waste products.

The words "hollow" and "solid" as they are normally understood don't quite fit here. I'm not sure of the right words or scientific concepts I need to properly express this, but the moon and the sun also have such "channels," which allow them to function properly. These also keep the sun from expanding too much or burning too quickly. When these channels function smoothly, the life of planets and suns is long, but when they don't, their life becomes shortened. How well these function depends upon how we use our minds. It is like this because our minds and the universe are linked together. How well we use our minds is also what determines whether pollution harms us or not.

I rarely spoke of these things in the past because people have a hard time accepting them. Instead, they tended to just call me crazy and ignore what I was saying. This also happened when I said that the Earth and moon are both "hollow," and that it was a significant misunderstanding to think of them as being utterly filled with solids or liquids.

Beings once lived on Mars as well, but the air disappeared and made it impossible to live there. This happened as the pollution became severe. But lives are gradually appearing now, because our minds have the ability to cause life to appear or to disappear. Likewise, if we want water to be there, it gradually appears. You all have the freedom to do this. Don't disregard yourself. If you look down upon yourself, it's the same as looking down upon the fundamental Buddha-nature that's been guiding you. We can't just continue to live and die in ignorance of our fundamental nature. Dying isn't the problem. The real problem is that, first, if everyone continues on like this, eventually the whole world will have to start over from the cold, harsh beginning. Second, if you die without knowing that everything is one, that everyone's parents are your own parents, you won't see any improvement in your next life. From the very beginning, throughout our entire evolution, we've always been connected to every other life. My parents aren't separate from your parents – everyone has been our parents, our children, our brothers, and our sisters.

If you are someone who is able to rely upon your fundamental mind, then your name is already known throughout the universe and the upper realms. Some of your faces say that you think I'm making all of this up, but I'm not. It is really true. Not everything that is written down and recorded is visible to your eyes.

Again, I can't emphasize enough how important it is to learn to rely upon our fundamental mind. When some of our sunims were visiting Pompeii, they were asked for help by the spirits of those who died by fire and drowning a very long time ago. So the sunims stayed up all night trying to help them. When they came back and told me this, I said, "Why was staying up all night necessary? Look at the water in this cup; if it's added to the sea, it becomes the sea. All those spirits can become your mind in an instant, so what's left to do? Mind has no limitation. Offerings of fruit or flowers – anything at all – can be done through mind.

Practicing like this, you can help free the spirits of the dead, but there's something that's even more important: While practicing with the things that come up in your life, and learning to entrust them to your fundamental mind, you can also protect this place we live in and ensure that it flourishes for a long time. Practicing like this, you'll continue to raise your spiritual level, and reach the point where the brightness you've attained will never, ever fade.

A sunim asked why, unlike other temples, we don't have huge tables of food when we have a ceremony to help the dead. I answered that for eons we've struggled to eat, to obtain, and to dig, all the while fighting and dying, and constantly getting a new body. So in order to help dissolve these states of consciousness, you should just put those spirits into the energy of the universe and tell them to eat as much as they want, and to do whatever they would like to. If you can do this, helping the dead is very straightforward. It's not complicated if you truly understand that everything is constantly changing and flowing as one whole. To put it bluntly, if you can freely use the infinite energy that always surrounds us, there's no need for table after table of offerings.

Our sunims go through so many hardships when they build a new Dharma hall, don't they? So much sincerity and good intention goes into the construction process and finding just the right Buddha statue. All of this is to help teach people that the mind of Buddha can become one with you and I.

The Spiritual and Material Realms are One

As we practice, we're trying to take care of the things in our lives while being grounded in the spiritual realm. However, sometimes this causes people to make the mistake of looking down upon the material realm. As you reflect upon yourself, all of you probably understand that the material and spiritual realms work together as one. Without consciousness, your body would be just a corpse. And if you didn't have a body, what could your consciousness do? How could you lead a normal existence unless the spiritual realm and the material realm were functioning as one combined whole?

Nonetheless, people think that Buddhas exist apart from themselves, that the spiritual realm exists apart from the material realm, and that the Buddha's body exists apart from our body. But all of this is wrong. Know that the body of Buddha is your own body. Know that the mind of Buddha is your own mind. Know that the truth the Buddha taught exists throughout every part and instant of your daily life. Further, know that if you are in pain, the whole knows of your pain. Everyone is your parent; everyone is your own child. So, don't get caught up in the trap of discriminations. This is also what Sakyamuni Buddha taught.

You know, as I think about it, my lack of education has worked out really well for all of you! If I'd had an education, I might be trying to explain this in terms of theory, with all kinds of long, scholarly words. Instead, because I never went to school, I can speak to you directly, in terms we can all understand. I'm like a village farmer who doesn't know how to beat around the bush! [Laughs.]

There are many, many things happening with our world and universe, and most of them I can't reveal to you because people aren't ready to hear about them. Perhaps later, when you can digest this, I can say more about them. Even among the things I've mentioned, some people worry that if we talk about those, or think too much about them, then our words and thoughts will cause those harmful things to come true. However there's no need to worry about such things when you understand this beautiful, non-dual practice, for it can handle all problems, even those of the living and the dead.

When I talk about these things, I can feel that many people can't take in what I'm saying. So I usually don't want to talk too much about them because I'm concerned that people will think

I'm crazy, and so won't try to practice. The current situation is quite urgent; everyone needs to work on their practice until they are able to understand and respond to these issues. Don't turn away from these problems, excusing yourself with a "well, it's beyond my understanding...."

Look at what happens on an individual level: among all the many different kinds of seeds, one begins to raise its level and peels off its shell time after time. Even though it was stuck in the dirt, it became a great pear tree that eventually reached the heavens, and has five great, golden pears hanging from it. Did that pear tree grow into such a magnificent tree by tearing apart and eating other living beings? No. It grows uprightly, and those huge pears can swallow even the universe. Now what would you think if I told you that the tree and those pears were you yourself?

There's nothing in the universe that can replace trees like these. If you can become such a tree, you can move the entire world using nothing more than the tiniest of things. At this point, you will be a practitioner who functions throughout the unseen realm, and a scientist who brings forth what is needed into the visible realm. This is vastly beyond the abilities of those scientists who do everything based upon only the material realm. Even when they can see something starting to happen, they can't do anything about it.

If you could foresee that a cup of water is about to fall and break, is that enough? What you should do is prevent it from happening. Although this may seem hard to believe, please keep in mind that all of you have the ability to do this. Even small and trivial things begin at the unseen realm and then manifest into the visible world. Likewise, our reactions to everything we see, hear, and feel are all input into the unseen realm.

This is why I keep saying that we have to remind ourselves that no matter the circumstances we find ourselves in – pleasant or difficult, whether we are awake or asleep – they are all being done by our fundamental mind. You all are the ones who can make this world into a wonderful place to live, and you are the ones who can save all the life on this world. And I don't mean just those beings who come to you looking for help. You are the one who can save all beings, even those who don't know they're stuck. If you can quietly work through the unseen realm to help them evolve, and can do this without talking or boasting about it, you will definitely receive an award from the Earth, as well as the universe!

Are there no questions today? No one has anything to ask? Whether your question seems stupid or not, if it's a question that wells up from within you, then that's a true question. If you overthink it and try to come up with a "good" question, that will actually be a fake question. And if you ask me a fake question, you may get a fake answer! [Laughs.]

We all go through difficult times of illness, loneliness, hopelessness, stress, frustration, and even times when you wish you could die. But we are nonetheless alive here now. So, we may as well live wisely. What do you all think! [She puts her palms together in front of her.] So, no one wants to ask me why I talk about such strange things? [Laughs.] Sometimes people call me crazy, but it's the whole world that's doing crazy things. People's behavior is steadily worsening as the situation around the world becomes more desperate. This is why we need to deepen our practice to the point where we can just smile even if the heavens come crashing down.

If there are no questions, do you want to hear about the overseas branches? Okay. [She looks around.] When I was in Canada, there was a newspaper photographer who followed me everywhere, even when I went on a trip to the mountains. But he was always very considerate about taking photos. I don't see him today, but then again, I wouldn't be surprised to hear that he's at the airport now!

Ah, I forgot to tell you about the German Dharma talk. It went very well, with over two hundred people attending, including the Korean Ambassador. In Germany, people aren't used to seeing Buddhist nuns or monks, so wherever we went they would stop and stare at us. So, I smiled at one group and told them that if they were going to stare at us, then they should pay us something for having entertained them. Hearing the translation, those serious-looking people laughed so hard they almost cried!

At the talk we used a new system of simultaneous translation, which worked very well. The German center also looks very nice. There's small, square garden in the center of the house that's open to the sky and is almost a small courtyard. It's surrounded by glass walls, so you can sit in the house and look out at it. It was nice to watch the trees blow in the wind. The center is very pretty and has a large yard and garden next to the Dharma hall.

In Canada, we bought the building that used to be the center for the Korean Immigrants Association, and the space is huge! The newly installed Buddha statue was so pure and bright! The building also came with a huge parking lot. So, for the opening they covered it with awnings and about 1,400 people came to hear the Dharma talk.

People from many different countries attended, and there were a lot of people who had some sense of living through our fundamental mind. One fellow wearing a turban asked me who created the universe. I said it was four guys named Fire, Water, Earth, and Air, who got together and created the world. [Laughs.]

He could understand my answer because I don't have any education. If I'd gone to school and was able to explain all of the deep meanings of this using the proper scientific and technical terms, people would have no idea what I'm talking about. [Laughs.] If I'd used the technical terms, people probably would have misunderstood me. Instead, I answered him very simply and directly, and when he heard my full answer, he clapped and raised his hands in the air.

If you want to attain something, then do it in a big way, so that you can truly make a difference in the world. Take everything in the entire world and utterly put it into this one place [holding up one finger]. And take all those trivial things and throw them away. Don't worry about the things you let go of to this unseen place; they're still yours. [Laughs.]

Let's stop here for today; if I go on about my trip, we won't have anything fun to talk about next time!

Protecting The Earth

This Dharma talk was given by
Daehaeng Kun Sunim on August 4, 1991.

August 4, 1991

BUDDHA-NATURE IS THE ESSENCE OF THE UNIVERSE

It has been a couple of months since we've been able to meet like this, so I'm happy to see everyone again.

Looking around at this world we've been born into, it's clear that through our minds and actions, and observing the workings of these, we can develop ourselves and look after the planet. In fact, it's not an exaggeration for me to say that we could be the guardians of the Earth. If we want to be able to take care of our own country, as well as global problems, and create the conditions for growth and a peaceful future, then we have to firmly give rise to those specific thoughts. However, if we use our minds unwisely, then, instead of peace, we will experience suffering and ugliness.

As I am sure you know, if we start excluding things, we are no longer talking about Buddhism or the Buddha-dharma. The whole of your existence is Buddhism. Not a single one of you, not a single thing in the universe can be excluded from this. The first part of the word Buddhism, "Bul"(佛) in Korean, means the Buddha-nature that every single one of you has. The second part, "gyo"(敎), refers to the interactions and communications that happen between us. When we meet, we automatically interact with each other, don't we? All of you are Buddhism, and everything in the universe is also Buddhism. Today on the mountain, I met up with a pine tree that I often see. Although it's a different day and we talked about different things, each time we meet, we're connecting and communicating with each other.

Although it's obvious that you and I have different bodies and different lives, we are connected as one through our foundation; thus, our minds are always able to communicate with each other and work together as one. However, if we don't know that we are always functioning together as one, through our foundation, then we are like a house that's been left empty and abandoned. It's like we're constantly being robbed and having our energy stolen. Because of this, there are many people who lose out in their lives. If you're like an empty house, if your energy is always being lost, then your body can easily be ruined, your mind becomes impoverished, and it will be very hard to live a fearless and upright life. When things come to this point, harmony and peace will be strangers in your home. When a tree's root is unhealthy, how could the leaves and branches ever flourish?

The Buddha-dharma isn't separate from any one of us. It's functioning there in every single thing we do. "Buddha" refers to our eternal Buddha-nature, which is the eternal foundation of all life, and which has infinite ability. We all have the ability such that if we raise thoughts, they will manifest into this world, and this is called "Dharma." Even though we have evolved into human beings, if we don't use this ability to raise thoughts, how can we call ourselves humans?

Energy is flowing throughout everything in the universe, always coming and going, being used and transformed into other forms of energy. This is how the entire universe works. Think about this: Sakyamuni Buddha took uncountable beings and became one with them all. He didn't exclude even a single one. He gathered them all together within one mind, which is the place beyond all names and fixed forms. He put them all here, so it's not an exaggeration to say that he combined them with the energy of the entire universe. If, from this combined energy, you give rise to a thought, it will manifest into the world. This whole process is what we call "turning the Dharma Wheel."

When our clothes are frayed and worn out, we throw them away and replace them with new clothes. Human beings do this, and stars do as well. When their body is worn out, they take it off and replace it with a new one. The only difference is the length of their lives. Taking off your clothes isn't dying. Why? Because Buddha-nature remains. Everything that we are scatters and returns to its basic elements, and yet remains just as it is; thus, we say that there is no death. When the conditions are right, Buddha-nature just gathers and takes shape as a new body. This is like when old, beaten-up gold is put into a furnace. It comes back out as rings and necklaces and such, but it is still gold. Likewise, no matter what happens, Buddha-nature is there.

Even though this Buddha-nature is inherent within all of us, just having Buddha-nature is not enough. There has to be practice and application. Only then will it be possible for you, through the foundation, to become one with everything. Working together like this, energy is sent out in all different forms. This is turning the Dharma Wheel. In this way, everything, including ourselves, is reborn through this great whole.

Let Go and Let Go of Your Thought Habits

If we turn our back on this practice, we can't move beyond where we are now. We'll be stuck in the same state. Even after death, you'll be caught up in the ideas you had while alive, and will mistakenly think you're still carrying around a body. If you die without having brightened your mind, you won't be able to move past those ideas. So, you'll think that you have the same shape as you did while alive, you won't know where you are supposed to go, and won't be able to take even a single step forward. To put it another way, all of the good and bad karma that you've planted will fill the world around you, and chase after you like your own shadow. So, you won't be able to move even an inch forward. This is truly how things are, and what many people suffer through.

So I keep telling people to let go and let go of the thought habits they've made while living in the material realm; but I'm not saying that ordinary daily life is something to avoid. The truth exists throughout every part of your life. We live at the crossroads of breathing in and out, don't we? If you inhale, but can't exhale, you'll die, won't you? Likewise if you exhale, but can't inhale, you'll also die. If someone asks "Where is Buddha-nature?" or "Where is your foundation?" I'd answer, "You'll discover it in the midst of everything coming in and going out."

This is also the answer to the question, "What is it that perceives everything and responds?" In the old days, enlightened ones would remain silent, but would answer through mind, saying, "It is always there, perceiving and responding, bringing energy in and sending it out, and ceaselessly flowing." But teachers would still sometimes ask, "Where is Buddha-nature?" in order to see if practitioners had awakened to their inherent nature. Or they might ask, "Is going into the building the right way, or is leaving the building the right way? Is giving correct or is receiving correct?"

Anyway, the habits of thought and expectation that we've created while alive often stick with us even after death, and it's these that prevent us from moving forward. Why is this? First of all, people go through so much to have a family, a home, and money, so it can be very hard for them to let go of those attachments.

The second problem that prevents people from moving forward after they die is the habit of clinging to their children. Even while you're alive, your sons and daughters don't welcome meddling in their life, do they? Yet, once you lose your body, this habit of clinging will cause you to go around and interfere in all the things your children try to do. In doing this, you end up harming your children. People act like this because they don't realize that children are a continuation of themselves, and instead mistakenly think of children as someone separate from themselves. False discriminations like these give rise to all kinds of attachments. If parents can't let go of this kind of clinging while alive, it follows them after death, and often prevents them from moving forward.

Thirdly, even though someone has let go of attachments to their children, possessions, and family, the consciousnesses of the lives that make up their body can still be a problem. If you haven't dissolved the collection of good and bad *karmic consciousnesses*[31] within your body, which have been created through cause and effect, then you'll have a very difficult time trying to step out from under the influence of those and go forward.

So, after you die, even though you want to move forward, those karmic states of consciousness continuously manifest before you, blocking your way. They appear and stick to you like your own shadow. Because you died without knowing the truth of nonduality and emptiness, you don't know how to handle those karmic states of consciousness as they continuously appear before you. Even though it looks like there is only a single pile of dog poop in front of you, you'll be hesitating because you're worried about stepping in it. So when it looks as if you're surrounded by terrible things in all directions, how could you move even an inch forward?

Or, you may be blocked by bad karma that you're carrying around. It may seem like you are being attacked by ghosts, with some missing eyes, others missing arms or legs, and still others with shapes that you couldn't have imagined while alive.

---

31. Karmic consciousnesses (業識): Kun Sunim has said that our behaviors, thoughts, and reactions to things are recorded as the consciousness of the lives within our body. Later, those consciousnesses arise one by one, replaying what was input. Thus we may feel happy, sad, angry, etc., without an obvious reason, or they may cause other problems to occur.

The way to dissolve these consciousnesses is to not react to them when they arise and to entrust them to our foundation. However, even these consciousnesses are just temporary combinations, so we shouldn't cling to the concept of them.

Everything about how you've lived during your past lives – what you did, what you said, and even thoughts you gave rise to – exists within you. After your physical body disappears, these karmic states of consciousnesses that you've created will continue to follow you around. So no matter where you go, there's no escape from them.

How can you move forward? If you completely shed those consciousnesses, you'll be free to go. However, as long as you're caught by them, they permeate your awareness, and stick with you like your own shadow. No matter what you achieve, no matter how far you've come, they're still there with you. Even when you return again to this world, those karmic consciousnesses are still following you. Only when we are free from those consciousnesses will we be free from being bothered or perceived by the unseen realms.

These karmic states we carry around cause us to constantly be followed and judged. It's as if the head of an intelligence agency has turned all of his agents loose on us. Imagine that the *Tusita Realm*[32] is carefully examining everything you do. How could you escape this kind of vigilance? All the evidence is recorded within your fundamental mind, which

---

32. Tusita Realm (兜率天)**:** This is traditionally described as one of six Deva Realms, that is, realms of beings who are more developed than ordinary people. It is said that humans can reach it through meditation, and it is also where Sakyamuni Buddha was said to reside prior to his being born on Earth.

However, Daehaeng Kun Sunim describes the Tusita Realm as the dimension that nurtures and prepares every single thing and then sends it out into the world. This entire universe is working as one, interconnected whole, and the Tusita Realm is the dimension where we can connect with this flowing whole and can instantly communicate with everything in the universe. Here we can freely use and direct the infinite energy of the whole.

We have to awaken and then attain the freedom to do this. Then we can live as a truly free person, and also fulfill the true role of a Bodhisattva.

is always communicating with the Tusita Realm, so it clearly sees everything you've recorded. Even if you were to run for five hundred years, you couldn't escape from the eyes of the Tusita Realm. The only way to free yourself from this is to keep entrusting and entrusting whatever arises back to your foundation.

Take whatever comes out and return it back to the place it arose from. When you do this, then things are not being done by "me"; rather, they're being done by the foundation. Our foundation is aware of everything and is actually doing everything. Ultimately, it is what guides us, and we just run errands for our foundation.

So, entrust everything to Juingong, knowing that, "Juingong is the one that's doing all of this, so it's the one that can take care of all of this." In this way, you can be completely free from those karmic consciousnesses. However, instead, people go around thinking they are the ones who are doing everything, and are filled to the brim with thoughts of "I." Furthermore, so much was input in the past, which is now constantly coming back out. Yet instead of dissolving this, people keep repeating it again and again. This is such a shame.

All of that will come back to them in the future. Nothing will change. You need to understand that everything you do is automatically recorded within you. As soon as those things come back out into the present, you have to return them to your foundation. If you can do this, those previous recordings will be utterly erased. Then, to return to my previous example, even if those intelligence agents examine you to your very core, there's nothing left for them to grab onto. You'll be completely free from karmic consciousnesses.

Once you understand this principle of emptiness, you should go forward letting go – to your foundation – all the things you encounter in your everyday life. Even now, what you see, hear, do and encounter, all of these are constantly flowing. Nothing of them remains behind, nothing of them remains unchanging. Every part of them has already flowed away. When you realize this, you won't allow clinging, anxiety, or emotional pain to settle within you. We are supposed to eat and then excrete, eat and excrete again. This may sound trifling, but this is exactly how our world is working. If you're willing to let go of the things people normally chase after, and if you completely understand the nature of that which you've been calling "me" and "I," then you'll discover that within you lies the ability to perceive and control all the things of this world.

Truly, Put your Practice Into Practice

You all have this ability, so this is where you need to focus your attention. Don't get lost in other people's theories. Those are useless to you. If you aren't working at putting this ability into practice, then when you desperately need this clear spring water, you won't be able to take even a sip. Even though your body is withered and exhausted, you won't be able to refill your energy. You have to know that, "Everything, including all my health problems, arises from within one mind, so within one mind is where it has to be solved. If I realize that me and my true self aren't separate, then I can do a good job of running errands."

Even just this thought, entrusted to your foundation, will cause energy to flow into your body, and illnesses caused by a lack of energy will naturally disappear. Further, when you practice like this, all of the different lives that make up a disease become one with you. Each becomes "myself." These countless forms of myself won't hurt myself. Would fingers on the same hand hurt each other? No.

As long as you're still controlled by karmic consciousnesses, you can't take even one step forward. No matter how far you run away, they'll still haunt you like a demon. Even after you leave this life and are later reborn, you'll still end up at the state that represents the level of your thoughts and behaviors during your past life. Thus you have to raise your level, and the way to do this is by continuously entrusting every single thing to your foundation. Have faith that all things are being done by your foundation, entrust it with everything, and so free yourself.

Although it may seem like you are completely free from those consciousnesses, if even a little residue of them remains, the idea of "me" will still remain, as will your habits. This means that, after death, if it looks like the path you need to take crosses a river, you will be scared that the water is too deep or too fast, and so won't be able to get across it. If your spirit tries instead to wait for a boat to take it to the other side, it could easily waste five hundred lifetimes or more waiting for something to show up. So, you have to completely let go. In Buddhism, there is a mantra that says, "Let's cross the hills, and there on the other side of the river, let's meet up. There, on the other side of these, we can find the vast, eternal light." This is the meaning of the Sanskrit verse, "Gate, gate, paragate, parasamgate bodhi savaha."

If you want to be able to cross over those hills and rivers and experience this light, then you need to input the thought that "Everything, all matter and energy, and every single form of life is not separate from myself. None of the lives that make up this body are separate from me. Everything is connected with me, nothing exists apart." I've told you this many times in the past because this is so important for you to understand. Nothing is separate from anything else, so if you take one thing by itself, you can't see its true identity. If you deeply understand this, you will know what is meant by "Dreaming is being awake and being awake is dreaming." If you are awake now, then you will be awake in dreams and awake after death.

If your eyes have thus awakened and your ears have opened, then with one thought, even fearsome rivers and endless plains will no longer bother you. You may be confronted by mountains so high you can't cross them, or plains that never come to an end, or rivers so deep and fast they would drown anyone, or wall of fire that threaten to burn you to ash. Yet with a single thought, these will all disappear. However, if you haven't been completely letting go of your fixed ideas, then although you may be able to get past some of these obstacles, you may find yourself blocked by others. For example, you may get past the mountains, only to find yourself waiting for a boat that will never come.

You are Buddha-nature

This entire universe – everything in it and all matter – is Buddha-nature. Stars are Buddha-nature, and human beings are Buddha-nature. Buddha-nature is functioning as one interconnected whole. This combined functioning absorbs everything like a black hole or a whirlpool of energy. Look at stars, planets, and comets. Some are huge and others tiny, aren't they? They're always coming into existence, and disappearing, while splitting into pieces, spreading out, gathering, and forming new shapes. The entire whole and everything in it is functioning like this, but if you don't know this, and limit your perspective to only a very narrow view of things, then you will be unable to fill the role of a great being. You'll only be able to play a role of a bellboy, forced to spend your life running around doing small, trivial jobs. It will be very hard for you to move beyond this level as long as you remain unaware of how the whole is working. Likewise, if you can't completely let go, you won't be able to enter the whirlpool of energy because it will look like a wheel of fire, and you'll be afraid of being burned to death. Thus, you won't have even the slightest taste of enlightenment. You won't be able to attain the freedom that is this eternal brightness. If you can realize this eternal brightness, you'll be a truly free person, someone who isn't pushed around by the cycle of life and death.

Although we talk about a lot of different things here, underlying all of them is mind. There is so much Buddha-nature! Everything exists as Buddha-nature. This is the base that makes it possible for us to raise thoughts. Sometimes this base, Buddha-nature, is also called mind. Of course, Buddha-nature and mind aren't exactly the same thing.

Buddha-nature is the essence of our life and has made it possible for us to be born. It's also the foundation that makes it possible for us to give rise to thoughts, and it's the foundation that makes it possible for those thoughts to function throughout the world, when we entrust them. Functioning through our Buddha-nature, those thoughts manifest into the world and become Dharma, so it's said that Buddha-nature and Dharma are inseparable. If you have this foundation of life, you can give rise to thought, and then your body and the material world will move accordingly.

I can't stress enough how important it is for you to free yourself from the kinds of attachments and fixed ideas that I mentioned earlier. If you don't do this, then things you've input will continuously come back out and prevent you from living freely. If you don't erase that input, no matter how far you run away, it will still find you and cause you to experience the results of what you've input. You'll be stuck in a prison with invisible walls and bars. In this prison, it's your mind and spirit that are trapped and can't move freely. A further problem is that you don't realize what's happened to you. You think you're still a physical being and that you can be affected by the things you see. Because you think those things have power over you, they do! And so you can't move forward.

Does anyone have any questions? The reason I ask this is because I'd like to have a free and open discussion. My sitting up here in the Dharma seat doesn't mean that I'm some sort of special person and you're people of lower standing. All it means is that we have a lot of people here, and those in the back won't be able to see me otherwise! However, I have been – and am even now – working in countless ways through this fundamental mind. You shouldn't disregard this, yet nor should you worship this flesh of mine. Do you know what kind of work all of the great Seon Masters and the Buddhas have done? Their greatest role was the ceaseless work they did through the unseen realm, the unseen fifty percent of reality. You all have heard these teachings, but have you tried to put them into practice like that?

Wisely Taking Care of Things

Mind doesn't exist as physical thing, so if you deeply awaken and are able to apply this mind of ours, then as you become one with whatever you encounter, you will be able to take care of everything, for the thoughts you give rise to will be freely manifest into the world. This is called the "Seven Treasures of Living Emptiness." Not only will you be able to greatly help others, you'll also help take care of issues related to planets and the universe. There are some really interesting things about this, but if I were to tell you, you'd think I am crazy. Anyway, the important point is that you all need to learn to take care of things in the same way as the awakened ones and the Buddhas. You should be able to fit to whatever arises, small or large, and respond appropriately. Such is the way of the workings of mind, because this mind of ours is a flowing, living thing, able to manifest as anything.

Sometimes it is scientists who most quickly understand what I'm talking about. For example, energy is drawn towards a black hole, and gathers together there and then goes out and scatters again. Likewise, the Buddha-nature that is the eternal foundation of our mind gathers together and then scatters. In places and ways infinite beyond counting, it's constantly coming together and then separating. It's like breathing, like inhaling and exhaling. Our minds, too, are part of this flow, so we all have the innate ability to draw upon and use this energy as needed. When this energy manifests into the world, we can call this "turning the Dharma Wheel."

The energy we send out circulates and functions. And it also produces again something else. Think about how a child is born. First, parents mobilized this energy by giving rise to an intention and then applied it through action. If there had been no intention followed by action, how could a child have been born? I know this seems silly, but this is a very important point. Stars are born just like this. Stars, too, are born from this flowing energy of the whole. They also give off energy, and that energy gathers together through its common affinities and attractions. All of this is arising from the interconnected functioning of the whole; it isn't something that just happens randomly or separately from everything else. It's all interconnected, because energy doesn't exist as a fixed form.

If we look at this energy as a whole, it isn't increasing or decreasing, because it's being regulated by the controlling and balancing effect of our fundamental mind. If this was missing, that energy might expand wildly, for example, and the results would be disastrous beyond imagining. Even science doesn't have the words to describe how bad things would be.

Anyway, you have to start by escaping from "me" and "I." This is the most important thing. If you can do this, you won't leave behind any traces of what you've done, i.e., you won't be creating karmic echoes. If you're not free from this "I," then whatever you do will leave behind traces and karmic consciousnesses that constrain you. How could you then freely go forth throughout all realms, both seen and unseen, and fulfill the roles of an awakened one? You'll be left behind, struggling in an invisible prison. That's why the Buddha said, "Escape, escape, be free from this prison of suffering."

Take Some Time to Reflect Upon Yourself

What else is there to say? I've explained everything about this, so I hope that you've grasped the key points by now. Please think carefully about what I've said. If, while working, you happen to remember something from a Dharma talk, take that and apply it to what's confronting you, and then entrust that situation to your foundation. If you have a chance, set aside some time to think about these things. If you don't reflect upon yourself, your mind won't evolve; you won't be able to grow. If you don't think about any of these things, are you really a person? How are you different from a lump of rock or a piece of wood? How could there be any growth?

Look at all the lives within your body – these are the evidence of where we've evolved from. You feel good if you go for a walk in the mountains, or if you stop and watch flowing water, don't you? Everyone enjoys this, because it's your home. You feel refreshed when you see the green mountains or when you watch fish playing in the water. These places were your home, where you've come from. Those are shapes you've had during the kalpas it has taken to evolve into a human being. We all lived as beings that crawl the earth, and as beings that walk around on four legs. Even now, we still have a bit of tailbone remaining. Yet we have to continue to evolve and be free from the control of these older consciousnesses; then we won't leave any traces behind us. We'll be able to live according to the thoughts we give rise to and won't be entangled by the past habits of the body. We'll be able to taste the world in which we can take care of everything through our thoughts. We've already evolved up to the human level, so shouldn't we go a bit further and taste this world of the mind?

Sometimes when I go for a walk, I see a type of crawling bug that looks something like a worm or small snake; I don't know what it's actually called. Anyway, it spawns eggs, attaches them to its rear, and then drags them to a safe place. There, it makes a thick bed of grass, places the eggs on top, and covers them with a light layer of grass. I'm always amazed when I see this. It's so marvelous, and is just one example of the incredible things we've been doing in the course of evolving into human beings. Throughout this whole process, from microbes until now, parents feed and clothe their children, and tuck them into bed. So, even now, when children are out late, parents become restless, "Why aren't they home yet?" When I think about the attachments parents have to children, it seems to me that we're still under the influence of these earlier levels.

Family, Wisdom, and Nonduality

Over the course of eons, we've gathered together and then scattered like leaves in the wind. We gather together as members of one family, scatter, and then gather as members of another family. If we've evolved a bit, we gather together with a more evolved family. If we've devolved a bit, well…. We've been going through this time after time. Thus, broadly speaking, "parents" and "children" are just temporary ideas. In any particular life, we've just gathered together for a short time. So instead of getting possessive, treat them with love.

However, most parents respond with rage when their son or daughter stays out all night, "Where did you spend the night?! Who were you with?! Give me their number!" If you act like this, they will become much more defiant, and will grow further apart from you. Try to assume that there were unavoidable circumstances, and ask them if they've eaten. If you can embrace them with a warm heart, they won't leave even if you try to kick them out! Nonetheless, because of parents' fixation on their children, they often yell and scold them. Parents should treat their children with respect, but often they act as if their children are some kind of possession. This is why some parents behave badly.

Every one of your children was once an adult who grew old and died, and has now been born again as a child. All of you have grown old and died, and been born as children. The only difference is that this time you are slightly older than them. [Laughs.] Even though you gave birth to them, don't view them as something you own. They are not your possessions. They don't belong to you! Further, whether they're your children or someone else's children, your parents or someone else's, treat them all as you would treat yourself. If you see someone in need, if you hear about someone who is suffering, just help them. If material help is needed, and you have enough to spare, then give that. If you don't, then be sure to help them through mind. Actually, helping someone through mind like this is really a great thing. Just make sure it's something that leaves them better off. Then it will be something wonderful.

Sometimes students visit me, crying and asking for help with problems involving their parents. At that moment, how could someone not see them as their own children? You have to see all children equally, as your own children, and then you can truly love them. It's the same for material things. You can't truly share them or give them to someone else as long as you view them as "mine." Instead, you'll always be expecting something in return or making demands upon the other person. These expectations and demands keep people from being able to open their heart and step out of their narrow ideas. My heart aches when I see young people crying because of such things. Sometime they've been your children, sometimes they've been my children. Sometimes they've been my parents, sometimes they've been your parents. We gather together and then scatter in the breeze. We're like wanderers who come together for a picnic, and then go our separate ways when night falls. This is the truth of our life. Please think about this when you have some quiet time.

I've spoken for a long time, so now you need to speak so that I can learn something! We all take turns sharing and learning from each other. Sometimes I'll speak to a flower or plant, and other times I'll be just quietly looking at them when they'll start speaking to me. Think about this: even flowers often close up for the nights. Some of you have seen this, haven't you? As their petals close for the night, do you know what they say? They say, "The sun has set. Whew. Let's get some sleep." Whereas the great pines are often awake, so there's a lot of meaning in them being called "evergreen." Some other plants and trees live like this as well. This kind of understanding comes from communicating with our hearts, through our fundamental mind.

There was a man who was destined to be killed by a falling tree. But he realized that trees also have an essence or "spirit," and began thinking of them as friends and good company, inwardly speaking kindly to them. Although he was destined to be killed by a tree, because he had been viewing the trees as one with himself, instead of hurting him, the spirits of those trees protected him from harm. Let me give you an example: If the head of a huge company truly feels that he and the employees are all in it together, and come good or bad he shares what there is with them, treating them respectfully, how could they not appreciate that? Wouldn't they work diligently for someone like that? You and others don't exist separately.

So, if you can truly view others this way, no matter where you go, you will be okay. For the spirit of water becomes one with you, the spirit of trees becomes one with you, and the spirit of the earth becomes one with you. The Bodhisattvas Avalokitesvara and Ksitigarbha also become one with you. Everyone is one with you, everyone is yourself. Are there any questions today? Don't think that you already know everything. Let's talk and learn from each other.

Questioner 1(male): A bit ago, you told us that when the stars come to the end of their lives, they, too, change their clothes. Thinking about this and the Earth, I'm wondering where the Earth is at in terms of the aging process? Secondly, when did human beings first appear? Finally, in the sutras it says that beings are born in four ways, through moisture, eggs, wombs, and transformation. How were humans first born? Of course, now we are born through the womb, but what was it like to begin with? I'd appreciate your thoughts on this.

Kun Sunim: I've already spoken about the basics of this, but it seems like you couldn't make the connection. Look, although we're born through the womb, were the lives within us now born the same way? As an embryo, the lives that make up your body are constantly transforming, and then later the whole is born through the womb. Even at the very beginning, the consciousness of all of those other sperm cells transformed and combined with fertilized egg. Those consciousnesses stick to the embryo like a shadow and the whole is born through the womb. Even after we're born, the cells within us are continuously coming into existence through transformation. What more proof do you need that we're not born just through the womb? In terms of evolutionary development, we're only three years old. The earth too, is only three years old. Why? If you think carefully about I've said, you may have some idea. It's because human beings' way of living, and all beings really, has remained at about the same level! They are just walking in circles, without making much progress.

Let's see, you also asked me about when the stars change their shape. In the process of shedding their bodies, they churn and give off energy all around them. Every living thing moves, doesn't it? Shedding its body like this doesn't mean it's dying. It's just changing its shapes, going from, say, a triangle to a rectangle, to a pentagon to a hexagon. And just like us, they change as they age, sometimes ending up as very tiny stars.

The source of those stars' lives is also the source of our life. Could the Buddha-nature, that gave rise to us and makes it possible for us to live, be separate from those stars? No, we are all connected. Although our bodies live here on Earth, we are also living as stars. This sounds crazy, doesn't it? Yet, if your mind is small, your light will be small as well. If your mind is big, your light will also be big. When a great person is born, we say that a great star appeared, don't we? Also, when we see a shooting star, we say that someone died. When someone dies, their body scatters and they return to their source. The same thing happens to stars.

Think about the dirt under our feet. How did it come into being? Elements gathered together and formed it, right? Similarly, when we die, what happens to the elements that have formed our body? They all return back to their original form. This is why people say "Ashes to ashes, dust to dust." Even comets and meteors become dust that sometimes falls to the earth. Gathering and separating like this is what allows everything to live. How could we survive without dirt? Because of dirt we can live, and when we die, we become dirt that again gives rise to new life. The whole of the universe is functioning like this, giving and receiving, giving and receiving.

It's not an exaggeration to say that the whole universe is like a giant corporation with everyone working in different departments and offices. It feels like we are solidly sitting here, but actually we and this planet are floating in space. From the perspective of space, we might look like ticks or fleas clinging to the Earth, but that's not the case – we are the highest form of life on the Earth. Then why do we still seem to be living like parasites? It's because we can't exist without consuming materials from the Earth, but in the midst of living like this, we have evolved and risen above that level.

The reason our spiritual development hasn't been able to keep up with the times is that our consciousness has been too caught up in the material aspects of the world. Too many people are seeing others as separate from themselves. If they want something, they think they have to take it from someone else. They keep trying to get more than others, to eat more than others, to rise to a higher position than others, and so on. Trying to live like this causes endless suffering and hardships. This is why we have to practice and why we have to rise above this kind of level.

Take a look at stars and planets: their interactions are determined by the energetic states of the other surrounding stars and planets. Those with weaker energy will be influenced, controlled, or consumed by the stronger ones. It's automatic for them. This also happens with humans as well. If you don't have a grasp of your foundation, you can be affected by forces stronger than you. It's like how a large magnet sweeps up all of the smaller pieces of metal around it. Hmm, I can see that some of you don't believe me, but this is absolutely true. If some force stronger than you intended something negative, there's no limit to what it could do. And you couldn't even know what form the damage would take, because this "energy" can manifest in any possible form.

Likewise, if the people of Earth are unaware of their foundation, and don't know how to rely upon it, the Earth, too, could lose energy without limit. This happens not only between people, but also between people and animals, and it even happens between the planets and stars. If another planet or comet passes near the Earth, and there are no awakened practitioners, then the Earth could be damaged beyond repair. Even now, there are so many people and other beings living on the Earth that its energy has weakened a lot. Yet, if we deepen our spiritual practice and learn to apply the inherent ability of our true nature, we can create opportunities to refill the Earth's energy. In this way, it's possible to even extend the Earth's lifespan.

If you've really deepened your practice, all kind of things are possible. You've all heard how planets like Jupiter and Saturn are so extreme that life can't exist there, right? But they do have life – it's just asleep. If you've thoroughly awakened, and proved and tested your practice in the world around you, then you could also wake up those lives. But you couldn't do this if your understanding and ability was still hazy or you were overestimating your ability. If someone of insufficient ability did awaken those beings, the results would be horrible. Why? Because if you couldn't control them, these beings would live by consuming the spiritual essence of beings weaker and less developed than themselves. An empty shell is all that would be left of people who weren't practiced at relying upon their fundamental mind. This could happen regardless of how far away from us they are. Distances would mean nothing.

When I talk about things like this, some of you may think I'm a bit crazy. But the fact is, I don't really care what others think about me. I'm just peacefully going about my life, and having a bit of a laugh when people call me things like that. By the way, did you know that laughing keeps you from growing old? [Laughs.] If you really want to know whether what I'm telling you is true or not, practice diligently and grasp your fundamental mind. Then you will be able to see what I'm doing in the unseen realm. You'll be able to see that I'm not just this physical form, nor, at this moment, am I only in this one place.

If you fully awaken, such that you can take care of not only our world but the universe as well, then, should you need to wake up those sleeping beings, you can also create the conditions to sustain them, as well as all kinds of other life. And you can do this across many, many planets. It doesn't matter whether the planet is too hot or too cold if you have the ability to adjust that environment. The Buddha said that when it comes to transporting energy, ideas of "near" and "far" are irrelevant. When we want to move something from here to there, it doesn't have to be in just that form for the whole trip. If the form of that matter could be changed, then it would be much easier to transport, wouldn't it?

For example, if you need some substance from a tree, then you don't have to move the entire tree, you can take just that part and use it instead. Consider the matter of pregnancy: elements that are so small as to be almost invisible combine into one and form a life. Although their original form has disappeared, they are ceaselessly changing and working together, and create a living human being. So, what if you could take something that was a million times lighter than a single cell, and plant it on another world? If you take something from a hot world and add it to a cold world, that planet would warm up, wouldn't it? But being able to do this isn't really the issue. The main problem is whether you can control the beings that are awakened by this.

Although what I'm saying may seem kind of strange, I'm really quite a normal person. I don't talk about what I haven't experienced, nor do I waste my time on useless things. I'm telling you about these things because we are not separate. You all desperately need to learn how to rely upon your fundamental source and awaken! Then, in the coming times, you'll be able to save countless lives. We have to know about this fundamental mind of ours and be able to apply it for the benefit of those many beings who are as yet unaware of the miraculous workings of their own fundamental mind.

I'm not sure how much you'll understand of what I'm going to tell you now, but the lives within your body just follow whatever intention you give rise to, regardless of whether it's good or bad. If you want to steal something they all go along with that. And if you raise a good intention, that's what they work toward. They can't tell the difference between good and evil, so it's your job to train and guide them. In this way, they can be transformed into Bodhisattvas. Only after you're able to control and guide the lives within your own body will you be able to solve the problems of those lives that live on other planets. How could you hope to take care of beings who are far away when you can't even help the ones who are right in front of you?

I think that's enough about this for today; I seem to have gone on for quite a while. Let's see if anyone else has a question.

Questioner 2(male): There have been a lot of questions that I've wanted to ask you for some time, but now sitting here in front of you, they all seem kind of foolish.

Kun Sunim: Please don't get caught by thoughts, such as "foolish" or not.

Questioner 2: In the past you've said that if we don't have our *Jujangja*,[33] then we are like an empty house. There's something about this that I'd like to double check with you. I heard that if our minds are distracted or strongly chasing after outer things, then we become like an empty house and germs can invade our body, or our thinking can become very unclear and confused. I'd like to know what Jujangja is. Is this just an example of "skillful means," where the idea is something for us to cling to in order to help keep our minds grounded? Or perhaps, is Jujangja the

---

33. Jujangja (拄杖子)**:** Literally, a monk's staff, but often implied to mean a grasp or reliance upon our fundamental mind.

desire to practice and awaken, which becomes stronger the more I go to the Seon Center and the more I study the sutras? And yet other times I think Jujangja is the state where I'm feeling relaxed and calm, and my mind is unshakeable.

Kun Sunim: Wherever you go, whether it's a busy market or to the Seon Center, whether it's the quiet of your home or your work place, if you have firm faith that your fundamental mind is doing everything, then this is called Jujangja. It's this unshakeable, thoroughly grounded trust in your inherent nature. This centered mind is so wonderful! It's your treasure that you can use to do anything you want. You've always had it, but you lived without knowing this, so the things you did often went wrong, and all kinds of unwise thoughts arose. So, don't be deceived by these things. Learn to control your reactions to those, learn to unconditionally entrust everything that confronts you back to your fundamental mind.

Questioner 3(male): I had a question I wanted to ask you, but strangely enough, Jeong-nak Sunim answered it during the morning Dharma talk, and you, too, answered it in your talk just now. But I was reminded of another point I'm unclear about. Basically, where is our fundamental mind? As I was trying to practice, it occurred to me that in order to entrust anything to it, we must first discover it. But when I examine my six senses and the physical organs that correspond to these, I can't find anything at all.

Kun Sunim: Why are you trying to separate them? Don't they all belong to one body?

Questioner 3: I looked among those, hoping to find my fundamental mind, but I couldn't find anything. Also, while thoughts arise in my head and I think through my brain, you've sometimes told us, "Stop trying to understand through your head. Instead try to know, feel, and understand through your mind." Likewise, in Korea people usually point to their heart when they indicate their mind, but no matter how hard I tried, I couldn't find my mind there. Is our consciousness what is meant by "mind," or are mind and consciousness something different? I just don't have a clue where mind is or where I have to entrust things to.

Kun Sunim: What we call "mind" can easily tilt this way or that way, so it's important to gather all of our scattered thoughts into one place. Doing this allows us to go forward uprightly, and is what we mean when we say, in Korean, "Get a grip on yourself."

Mind doesn't exist outside of you, nor does it only exist within you. Thus, it can embrace the entire universe. If mind only existed within you, how could it embrace everything else? How could it function non-dually with everything in the universe? Because mind has no form and works as one with everything, in an instant Buddhas and Bodhisattvas can become one with you, give you amazing teachings, and then leave. Mind isn't something that you can see, touch, or grab hold of. It isn't something that exists only within your body or outside your body. Because of all this, mind can function in marvelous and profound ways, and it is possible for you to apply these vast and extraordinary principles of mind to do wonderful things. Without knowing how to truly apply your mind like this, could you become a Buddha? The mind that gives rise to thoughts right now, the mind that's speaking, seeing, asking questions, the mind that loves, hates – in all of this, there's nothing for you to grab hold of. Yet, it's through this very mind that you can become a Buddha.

Thus, it's said that you can find your fundamental mind as it functions throughout your daily life. Long ago in China, there was a Buddhist nun called Shi-ji(實際). She went to visit the monk Ju-zhi(俱胝), who had not yet awakened, but was serving as the abbot of a temple. She'd heard stories of him, and decided that she needed to go test him, and perhaps give him a push. He was sitting in the courtyard shelling peas when she walked in. She walked up to him, circled him three times, and then struck the ground with her staff. He just sat there, with no idea what she was doing. Shi-ji stood for a few moments, waiting for an answer, and then turned to leave. It was getting late in the day, so Ju-zhi, remembering his duties as abbot, offered her a room for the night. However, Shi-ji replied, "How can I stay where there are no people?" [34] With that, she left.

Ju-zhi just stared after her, feeling both dumbfounded and humiliated. After thinking about this some more, he decided to resign his position as abbot and go find some place where he could focus on his practice. He packed a small bag and prepared to leave the temple the next morning. That night, as he slept, he was told in a dream, "Don't leave. A good teacher will soon come to you." Before long a truly great teacher arrived at the temple, and with his guidance, Ju-zhi awakened. Later he became known as "Ju-zhi, of the one finger."

---

34. By this she meant "true people" i.e., awakened ones.

It's not possible for you to find your Jujangja, your centered mind, somewhere else. Because you raise your Jujangja, you're able to feel other's suffering, their joy, and to raise good intentions for them. Because you raise this firmly centered mind, it's possible for you to feel the desire to improve and become better. Only with this firmly centered mind can you do truly good things for others. Our mind is vast and boundless and manifesting in a thousand different ways; while there's no physical shape or feeling for us to grab onto, nonetheless, when we entrust everything that arises to our foundation, then in the middle of this, there arises something that we can rely upon: our Jujangja.

Because of the way this works, people sometimes say that form is emptiness, and emptiness is form. Because these don't exist apart, you can have the treasure that is your Jujangja or not, according to how well you entrust everything to your foundation. Thus, if you don't have this firmly centered mind, it's possible that others will come and take the place of your Jujangja – because anyone can freely enter an empty house. If you become like an empty house, the only thing that will prosper there will be spider webs. All sorts of problems will occur, whether they are caused by germs, genetics, or spirits. Imagine a bunch of trespassers in your house, dancing wildly, singing, and drinking themselves senseless. What kind of a state will your home be left in?

Are there any further questions? If not, let's stop here for today.

Glossary

Avalokitesvara Bodhisattva(觀世音菩薩): The Bodhisattva of Compassion, who hears and responds to the cries of the world, and delivers unenlightened beings from suffering.

Bhikkunis(nun): Female sunims who are fully ordained are called Bhikkuni(比丘尼) sunims, while male sunims who are fully ordained are called Bhikku(比丘) sunims. This can also be a polite way of indicating male or female sunims.

Bodhisattva: In the most basic sense, a Bodhisattva is a manifestation of Buddha, which helps save beings and also uses the non-dual wisdom of enlightenment to help them awaken for themselves.

Buddha: In this text, "Buddha" and "Bodhisattva" are capitalized out of respect, because these represent the essence and function of the enlightened mind. "The Buddha" always refers to Sakyamuni Buddha.

Buddha(佛), **Dharma**(法), **Sangha**(僧): Buddha means both the historical Buddha, as well as this fundamental enlightened essence. Dharma means both ultimate truth, and the truth taught by the Buddha. Sangha in its broadest sense means the community of great practitioners, both lay and monastic.

Cheondo(薦度): This involves helping the consciousness of the dead to move forward on their own path. It can happen that beings become "stuck" in their fears, attachments, and illusions, and so can't move forward. Cheondo often involves a special ceremony, but not necessarily, which in a sense educates the consciousness, and so allows it to move forward at a level that more accurately reflects the level they achieved while alive.

Clothes: In Korea, the word "clothes" is often used to describe our body. Like our body, they are something we take off at night (i.e. death), and then replace with a fresh set in the morning.

Five subtle powers(五神通): These are the power to know past and future lives, the power to know others' thoughts and emotions, the power to see anything, the power to hear anything, and the power to go anywhere.

Habits(習): These include not just the ways of thought and behavior learned in this life, but also all of those tendencies of thought and behavior that have accumulated over endless eons.

Hanmaum [han-ma-um]: "Han" means one, great, and combined, while "maum" means mind, as well as heart, and together they mean everything combined and connected as one. What is called "Hanmaum" is intangible, unseen, and transcends time and space. It has no beginning or end, and is sometimes called our fundamental mind. It also means the mind of all beings and everything in the universe connected and working together as one. In English, we usually translate this as "one mind."

Hwadu(話頭) (C. –hua-tou, J. –koan): Traditionally, the key phrase of an episode from the life of an ancient master, which was used for awakening practitioners, and which could not be understood intellectually. This developed into a formal training system using several hundred of the traditional 1,700 koans. However, hwadus are also fundamental questions arising from inside that we have to resolve. It has been said that our life itself is the very first hwadu that we must solve.

Ignorance(無明): Literally this means darkness. It is the unenlightened mind that does not see the truth. It is being unaware of the inherent oneness of all things, and it is the fundamental cause of birth, aging, sickness, and death.

Juingong(主人空): Pronounced "ju-in-gong." Juin (主人) means the true doer or the master, and gong (空) means "empty." Thus Juingong is our true nature, our true essence, the master within that is always changing and manifesting, without a fixed form or shape. Daehaeng Sunim has compared Juingong to the root of the tree. Our bodies and consciousness are like the branches and leaves, but it is the root that is the source of the tree, and it is the root that sustains the visible tree.

Jujangja(拄杖子): Literally, a monk's staff, but often implied to mean a grasp or reliance upon our fundamental mind.

Karmic affinity(因緣): The connection or attraction between people or things, due to previous karmic relationships.

Karmic consciousnesses(業識): Kun Sunim has said that our behaviors, thoughts, and reactions to things are recorded as the consciousness of the lives within our body. Later, those consciousnesses arise one by one, replaying what was input. Thus we may feel happy, sad, angry, etc., without an obvious reason, or they may cause other problems to occur.

The way to dissolve these consciousnesses is to not react to them when they arise and to entrust them to our foundation. However, even these consciousnesses are just temporary combinations, so we shouldn't cling to the concept of them.

Ksitigarbha Bodhisattva(地藏菩薩): The guardian of the earth who is devoted to saving all beings from suffering, and especially those beings lost in the hell realms.

Kyongho Sunim(鏡虛惺牛, 1846-1912) was the greatest Seon master of his era, and is responsible for much of the current vitality of Korean Buddhism. He had five great disciples, one of whom, Hanam Sunim, was Daehaeng Kun Sunim's teacher. Over fifty percent of the Buddhist monks and nuns in Korea can trace their lineage directly back to him.

Mind(心)(Kor. –maum): In Mahayana Buddhism, "mind" refers to this fundamental mind, and almost never means the brain or intellect. It is intangible, beyond space and time, and has no beginning or end. It is the source of everything, and everyone is endowed with it.

Mujeonja [/mu-jun-ja/]: The essence, or medium, that connects the material and non-material realms and allows them to function together harmoniously. It is the underlying essence that allows the balanced functioning of the non-material realm and what is manifested into the material realm. To put it another way, we call it something that allows the spiritual realms to freely interact with the material realm. If it had a physical essence, it couldn't perform this role, so it could be said that it belongs to the non-material realm. However, it is within the physical realm that the functioning of the mujeonja manifests, so we cannot say that it belongs to one realm or the other.

When the mujeonja manifests into the material realm, it works through a phenomena called "yujeonja"[/yu-jun-ja/]. Its movement gives the appearance of infinitely tiny threads, but it is so small that it's impossible to detect any mass. It's this yujeonja that gives rise to everything in our physical world, and makes it possible for everything to function and interact.

Noble Eightfold Path(八正道): Correct view, correct thought, correct speech, correct action, correct livelihood, correct effort, correct mindfulness, and correct concentration. Living in accord with these will lead one to enlightenment and make it possible to free other beings as well.

One Thought: This refers to the ability to raise and then input and entrust a thought to our foundation. When we can connect with our foundation like this, then through our foundation, that thought spreads to everything in the universe, including all of the lives in our body. At that instant, because all things are fundamentally not two, they all respond to that thought.

Precepts, Samadhi, and Wisdom(戒定慧): Traditionally described as the Threefold Training, these are aimed at putting an end to desire, hatred, and delusion. Precepts represent virtue and morality, samadhi represents transcendental awareness, and wisdom is this awareness in action.

Seon(Chan, Zen)(禪): Seon describes the unshakeable state where one has firm faith in their inherent foundation, their Buddha-nature, and so returns everything they encounter back to this fundamental mind. It also means letting go of "I," "me," and "mine" throughout one's daily life.

Six Paramitas(六波羅蜜): Charity, morality, restraint, effort, meditation, and wisdom. These are the six practices of a Bodhisattva, and when applied with a selfless attitude, will help free ordinary beings as well.

Sunim / Kun Sunim: Sunim is the respectful title of address for a Buddhist monk or nun in Korea, and Kun Sunim is the title given to outstanding nuns or monks.

Tathagata(如來): In one sense, Tathagata is just another name of the Buddha, meaning "Thus-come," but it also refers to the fully enlightened state that is able to both know and manifest with complete freedom.

Three Treasures(三寶): In their outer aspect, the Three Treasures are the Buddha, the Dharma, and the Sangha. Buddha means both the historical Buddha, as well as this fundamental enlightened essence. Dharma means both ultimate truth, and the truth taught by the Buddha. Sangha in its broadest sense means the community of great practitioners, both lay and monastic. These are also considered to have an inner aspect as well.

Tusita Realm(兜率天): This is traditionally described as one of six Deva Realms, that is, realms of beings who are more developed than ordinary people. It is said that humans can reach it through meditation, and it is also where Sakyamuni Buddha was said to reside prior to his being born on Earth.

However, Daehaeng Kun Sunim describes the Tusita Realm as the dimension that nurtures and prepares every single thing and then sends it out into the world. This entire universe is working as one, interconnected whole, and the Tusita Realm is the dimension where we can connect with this flowing whole and can instantly communicate with everything in the universe. Here we can freely use and direct the infinite energy of the whole.

We have to awaken and then attain the freedom to do this. Then we can live as a truly free person, and also fulfill the true role of a Bodhisattva.

Virtue and merit(公德): Here this term refers to the results of helping people or beings unconditionally and non-dually, without any thought of self or other. It becomes virtue and merit when you "do without doing," that is, doing something without the thought that "I did such and such." Because it is done unconditionally, all beings benefit from it.

Wonhyo Sunim(元曉, 617-686): A Silla dynasty monk who is considered one of Korea's greatest monks. Known for the depth of his enlightenment and penetrating wisdom, Wonhyo wrote numerous commentaries on the sutras, emphasizing that the different teachings of the various schools and sutras were merely different aspects of the same fundamental reality. All were based on the same underlying truth, and the variations were just reflections of the differences between eras, cultures, and people's ability to understand.

Books by Daehaeng Kun Sunim
-available through Hanmaum Publications

- Touching The Earth (English) (New)
- A Thousand Hands of Compassion (bilingual, Korean/English)
  [received *2010 iF communication design Award*]
- Wake Up And Laugh (English)
- No River To Cross, No Raft To Find (English)
- My Heart Is A Golden Buddha (English)
- *Practice in Daily Life* (Series) (bilingual, Korean/English)
  1. To Discover Your True Self, "I" Must Die
  2. Walking Without A Trace
  3. Let Go And Observe
  4. Mind, Treasure House Of Happiness
  5. The Furnace Within Yourself
  6. The Spark That Can Save The Universe
  7. The Infinite Power Of One Mind
  8. In The Heart Of A Moment (New)
  9. One With The Universe (New)
  10. Protecting The Earth (New)
- 건널 강이 어디 있으랴 (Korean)
- 내 마음은 금부처 (Korean)
- El Camino Interior (Spanish)
- Vida De La Maestra Seon Daehaeng (Spanish)
- Enseñanzas De La Maestra Daehaeng (Spanish)
- Práctica Del Seon En La Vida Diaria (Series)
  (bilingual, Spanish/English)
  1. Una Semilla Inherente Alimenta El Universo
- Si Te Lo Propones, No Hay Imposibles (Spanish)
- 人生不是苦海 (Traditional Chinese) (2014 New edition)
- 无河可渡 (Simplified Chinese)
- 我心是金佛 (Simplified Chinese) (New)

-Books available through other Publishers

- No River To Cross (Wisdom Publications, U.S.A.)
- Wake Up And Laugh (Wisdom Publications, U.S.A.)
- Wie Fließendes Wasser (Goldmann Arkana-Random House, Germany)
  German edition of *My Heart Is A Golden Buddha*
- Vertraue Und Lass Alles Los (Goldmann Arkana-Random House, Germany)
  German edition of *No River To Cross*
- Umarmt Von Mitgefühl (Diederichs-Random House, Germany)
  German edition of *A Thousand Hands Of Compassion*
- Wache Auf Und Lache (Theseus, Germany)
  German edition of *Wake Up And Laugh*
- Ningún Río Que Cruzar (Kailas Editorial, S.L., Spain)
  Spanish edition of *No River To Cross*
- 我心是金佛 (Oak Tree Publishing Co., Taiwan)
  Traditional Chinese edition of *My Heart Is A Golden Buddha*
- Дзэн И Просветление (Amrita-Rus, Russia)
  Russian edition of *No River To Cross*
- Sup Cacing Tanah (PT Gramedia, Indonesia)
  Indonesian edition of *My Heart Is A Golden Buddha*
- Không có sông nào để vượt qua (Phuong Nam Books, Vietnam)
  Vietnam edition of *No River To Cross*
- *No River To Cross* (title to be determined) (Sphinx Publishing, Egypt)
  Arabic edition of *No River To Cross*, Forthcoming 2015

한마음선원본원

경기도 안양시 만안구 석수동 101-62
Tel : 82-31-470-3100   Fax : 82-31-470-3116
홈페이지 : http://www.hanmaum.org   이메일 : jongmuso@hanmaum.org

국내지원

강릉지원 (우)210-952 강원도 강릉시 하평5길 29(포남동)
TEL:(033) 651-3003   FAX:(033) 652-0281

공주지원 (우)314-870 충청남도 공주시 사곡면 위안양골길 157-61
TEL:(041) 852-9100   FAX:(041) 852-9105

광명선원 (우)369-900 충청북도 음성군 금왕읍 대금로 1402
TEL:(043) 877-5000   FAX:(043) 877-2900

광주지원 (우)502-827 광주광역시 서구 운천로 204번길 23-1(치평동)
TEL:(062) 373-8801   FAX:(062) 373-0174

대구지원 (우)706-838 대구광역시 수성구 수성로 41길 76(중동)
TEL:(053) 767-3100   FAX:(053) 765-1600

목포지원 (우)530-490 전라남도 목포시 상동 952-19
TEL:(061) 284-1771   FAX:(061) 284-1770

문경지원 (우)745-823 경상북도 문경시 산양면 봉서1길 10
TEL:(054) 555-8871   FAX:(054) 556-1989

부산지원 (우)606-809 부산광역시 영도구 함지로 79번길 23-26(동삼동)
TEL:(051) 403-7077   FAX:(051) 403-1077

울산지원 (우)683-500 울산광역시 북구 달래골길 26-12(천곡동)
TEL:(052) 295-2335   FAX:(052) 295-2336

제주지원 (우)690-140 제주특별자치도 제주시 황사평6길 176-1(영평동)
TEL:(064) 727-3100   FAX:(064) 727-0302

중부경남 (우)621-802 경상남도 김해시 진영읍 하계로 35
TEL:(055) 345-9900   FAX:(055) 346-2179

진주지원 (우)660-941 경상남도 진주시 미천면 오방로 528-40
TEL:(055) 746-8163   FAX:(055) 746-7825

청주지원 (우)360-814 충청북도 청주시 청원구 교서로 109
TEL:(043) 259-5599   FAX:(043) 255-5599

통영지원 (우)650-110 경상남도 통영시 여황로 131(도천동)
TEL:(055) 643-0643   FAX:(055) 643-0642

포항지원 (우)791-813 경상북도 포항시 북구 우창로 59(우현동)
TEL:(054) 232-3163   FAX:(054) 241-3503

Anyang Headquarters of Hanmaum Seonwon

(430-040) 101-62 Seoksu-dong, Manan-gu, Anyang-si, Gyeonggi-do
Republic of Korea
Tel: (82-31) 470-3175 / Fax: (82-31) 470-3209
www.hanmaum.org/eng   onemind@hanmaum.org

Overseas Branches of Hanmaum Seonwon

ARGENTINA
Buenos Aires
Miró 1575, CABA, C1406CVE, Rep. Argentina
Tel: (54-11) 4921-9286 / Fax: (54-11) 4921-9286
www.hanmaum.org.ar

Tucumán
Av. Aconquija 5250, El Corte, Yerba Buena,
Tucumán, T4107CHN, Rep. Argentina
Tel: (54-381) 425-1400
www.hanmaumtuc.org

BRASIL
São Paulo
R. Newton Prado 540, Bom Retiro
Sao Paulo, CEP 01127-000, Brasil
Tel: (55-11) 3337-5291
www.hanmaumbr.org

CANADA
Toronto
20 Mobile Dr., North York, Ontario M4A 1H9, Canada
Tel: (1-416) 750-7943 / Fax: (1-416) 981-7815
www.hanmaumcanada.org

GERMANY
Kaarst
Broicherdorf Str. 102, 41564 Kaarst, Germany
Tel: (49-2131) 969551 / Fax: (49-2131) 969552
www.hanmaum-zen.de

THAILAND
Bangkok
86-1 soi 4 Ekkamai Sukhumvit 63
Bangkok, Thailand
Tel: (66-2) 391-0091
home.hanmaum.org/bangkok

USA
Chicago
7852 N. Lincoln Ave., Skokie, IL 60077, USA
Tel: (1-847) 674-0811
www.buddhapia.com/hmu/chi/

Los Angeles
1905 S. Victoria Ave., L.A., CA 90016, USA
Tel: (1-323) 766-1316
home.hanmaum.org/la

New York
144-39, 32 Ave., Flushing, NY 11354, USA
Tel: (1-718) 460-2019
Fax: (1-718) 939-3974
www.juingong.org

Washington D.C.
7807 Trammel Rd., Annandale, VA 22003, USA
Tel: (1-703) 560-5166
http://home.hanmaum.org/wa